C-4995

CAREER EXAMINATION SERIES

AF701387

THIS IS YOUR **PASSBOOK**® FOR ...

LABOR SPECIALIST TRAINEE

NLC®
NATIONAL LEARNING CORPORATION®
passbooks.com

NLC®

National Learning Corporation

212 Michael Drive, Syosset, NY 11791
(516) 921-8888 • www.passbooks.com
E-mail: info@passbooks.com

PUBLISHED IN THE UNITED STATES OF AMERICA

PASSBOOK® SERIES

THE *PASSBOOK® SERIES* has been created to prepare applicants and candidates for the ultimate academic battlefield – the examination room.

At some time in our lives, each and every one of us may be required to take an examination – for validation, matriculation, admission, qualification, registration, certification, or licensure.

Based on the assumption that every applicant or candidate has met the basic formal educational standards, has taken the required number of courses, and read the necessary texts, the *PASSBOOK® SERIES* furnishes the one special preparation which may assure passing with confidence, instead of failing with insecurity. Examination questions – together with answers – are furnished as the basic vehicle for study so that the mysteries of the examination and its compounding difficulties may be eliminated or diminished by a sure method.

This book is meant to help you pass your examination provided that you qualify and are serious in your objective.

The entire field is reviewed through the huge store of content information which is succinctly presented through a provocative and challenging approach – the question-and-answer method.

A climate of success is established by furnishing the correct answers at the end of each test.

You soon learn to recognize types of questions, forms of questions, and patterns of questioning. You may even begin to anticipate expected outcomes.

You perceive that many questions are repeated or adapted so that you can gain acute insights, which may enable you to score many sure points.

You learn how to confront new questions, or types of questions, and to attack them confidently and work out the correct answers.

You note objectives and emphases, and recognize pitfalls and dangers, so that you may make positive educational adjustments.

Moreover, you are kept fully informed in relation to new concepts, methods, practices, and directions in the field.

You discover that you arre actually taking the examination all the time: you are preparing for the examination by "taking" an examination, not by reading extraneous and/or supererogatory textbooks.

In short, this PASSBOOK®, used directedly, should be an important factor in helping you to pass your test.

LABOR SPECIALIST TRAINEE

DUTIES

An employee in this class is responsible for performing entry-level professional work within an assigned unit of the Department of Labor, Licensing and Consumer Affairs. The incumbent initially works under the close supervision of a Labor Specialist or higher level professional but is expected to perform with greater independence on routine matters as experience is gained. Duties include advising participants on employment and training, fieldwork programs, employment practices, business etiquette and available vocational training opportunities to aid them in gaining employment. The incumbent may assist Labor Specialists in supervising, monitoring and evaluating fieldwork activities of a crew of participants engaged in carrying out assignments at various sites within the County. Supervision is received from Labor Specialists or higher-level staff who review work through conferences and periodic inspections of activities. After one year of continuous service as a permanent Labor Specialist Trainee, the employee in this class achieves permanent competitive status as a Labor Specialist I without further examination. Does related work as required.

SCOPE OF THE EXAMINATION

The written test will cover knowledge, skills and/or abilities in such areas as:

1. Interviewing;
2. Understanding and interpreting written material;
3. Understanding and interpreting tabular material; and
4. Preparing written material.

HOW TO TAKE A TEST

I. YOU MUST PASS AN EXAMINATION

A. WHAT EVERY CANDIDATE SHOULD KNOW

Examination applicants often ask us for help in preparing for the written test. What can I study in advance? What kinds of questions will be asked? How will the test be given? How will the papers be graded?

As an applicant for a civil service examination, you may be wondering about some of these things. Our purpose here is to suggest effective methods of advance study and to describe civil service examinations.

Your chances for success on this examination can be increased if you know how to prepare. Those "pre-examination jitters" can be reduced if you know what to expect. You can even experience an adventure in good citizenship if you know why civil service exams are given.

B. WHY ARE CIVIL SERVICE EXAMINATIONS GIVEN?

Civil service examinations are important to you in two ways. As a citizen, you want public jobs filled by employees who know how to do their work. As a job seeker, you want a fair chance to compete for that job on an equal footing with other candidates. The best-known means of accomplishing this two-fold goal is the competitive examination.

Exams are widely publicized throughout the nation. They may be administered for jobs in federal, state, city, municipal, town or village governments or agencies.

Any citizen may apply, with some limitations, such as the age or residence of applicants. Your experience and education may be reviewed to see whether you meet the requirements for the particular examination. When these requirements exist, they are reasonable and applied consistently to all applicants. Thus, a competitive examination may cause you some uneasiness now, but it is your privilege and safeguard.

C. HOW ARE CIVIL SERVICE EXAMS DEVELOPED?

Examinations are carefully written by trained technicians who are specialists in the field known as "psychological measurement," in consultation with recognized authorities in the field of work that the test will cover. These experts recommend the subject matter areas or skills to be tested; only those knowledges or skills important to your success on the job are included. The most reliable books and source materials available are used as references. Together, the experts and technicians judge the difficulty level of the questions.

Test technicians know how to phrase questions so that the problem is clearly stated. Their ethics do not permit "trick" or "catch" questions. Questions may have been tried out on sample groups, or subjected to statistical analysis, to determine their usefulness.

Written tests are often used in combination with performance tests, ratings of training and experience, and oral interviews. All of these measures combine to form the best-known means of finding the right person for the right job.

II. HOW TO PASS THE WRITTEN TEST

A. NATURE OF THE EXAMINATION

To prepare intelligently for civil service examinations, you should know how they differ from school examinations you have taken. In school you were assigned certain definite pages to read or subjects to cover. The examination questions were quite detailed and usually emphasized memory. Civil service exams, on the other hand, try to discover your present ability to perform the duties of a position, plus your potentiality to learn these duties. In other words, a civil service exam attempts to predict how successful you will be. Questions cover such a broad area that they cannot be as minute and detailed as school exam questions.

In the public service similar kinds of work, or positions, are grouped together in one "class." This process is known as *position-classification.* All the positions in a class are paid according to the salary range for that class. One class title covers all of these positions, and they are all tested by the same examination.

B. FOUR BASIC STEPS

1) Study the announcement

How, then, can you know what subjects to study? Our best answer is: "Learn as much as possible about the class of positions for which you've applied." The exam will test the knowledge, skills and abilities needed to do the work.

Your most valuable source of information about the position you want is the official exam announcement. This announcement lists the training and experience qualifications. Check these standards and apply only if you come reasonably close to meeting them.

The brief description of the position in the examination announcement offers some clues to the subjects which will be tested. Think about the job itself. Review the duties in your mind. Can you perform them, or are there some in which you are rusty? Fill in the blank spots in your preparation.

Many jurisdictions preview the written test in the exam announcement by including a section called "Knowledge and Abilities Required," "Scope of the Examination," or some similar heading. Here you will find out specifically what fields will be tested.

2) Review your own background

Once you learn in general what the position is all about, and what you need to know to do the work, ask yourself which subjects you already know fairly well and which need improvement. You may wonder whether to concentrate on improving your strong areas or on building some background in your fields of weakness. When the announcement has specified "some knowledge" or "considerable knowledge," or has used adjectives like "beginning principles of..." or "advanced ... methods," you can get a clue as to the number and difficulty of questions to be asked in any given field. More questions, and hence broader coverage, would be included for those subjects which are more important in the work. Now weigh your strengths and weaknesses against the job requirements and prepare accordingly.

3) Determine the level of the position

Another way to tell how intensively you should prepare is to understand the level of the job for which you are applying. Is it the entering level? In other words, is this the position in which beginners in a field of work are hired? Or is it an intermediate or advanced level? Sometimes this is indicated by such words as "Junior" or "Senior" in the class title. Other jurisdictions use Roman numerals to designate the level – Clerk I, Clerk II, for example. The word "Supervisor" sometimes appears in the title. If the level is not indicated by the title, check the description of duties. Will you be working under very close supervision, or will you have responsibility for independent decisions in this work?

4) Choose appropriate study materials

Now that you know the subjects to be examined and the relative amount of each subject to be covered, you can choose suitable study materials. For beginning level jobs, or even advanced ones, if you have a pronounced weakness in some aspect of your training, read a modern, standard textbook in that field. Be sure it is up to date and has general coverage. Such books are normally available at your library, and the librarian will be glad to help you locate one. For entry-level positions, questions of appropriate difficulty are chosen – neither highly advanced questions, nor those too simple. Such questions require careful thought but not advanced training.

If the position for which you are applying is technical or advanced, you will read more advanced, specialized material. If you are already familiar with the basic principles of your field, elementary textbooks would waste your time. Concentrate on advanced textbooks and technical periodicals. Think through the concepts and review difficult problems in your field.

These are all general sources. You can get more ideas on your own initiative, following these leads. For example, training manuals and publications of the government agency which employs workers in your field can be useful, particularly for technical and professional positions. A letter or visit to the government department involved may result in more specific study suggestions, and certainly will provide you with a more definite idea of the exact nature of the position you are seeking.

III. KINDS OF TESTS

Tests are used for purposes other than measuring knowledge and ability to perform specified duties. For some positions, it is equally important to test ability to make adjustments to new situations or to profit from training. In others, basic mental abilities not dependent on information are essential. Questions which test these things may not appear as pertinent to the duties of the position as those which test for knowledge and information. Yet they are often highly important parts of a fair examination. For very general questions, it is almost impossible to help you direct your study efforts. What we can do is to point out some of the more common of these general abilities needed in public service positions and describe some typical questions.

1) General information

Broad, general information has been found useful for predicting job success in some kinds of work. This is tested in a variety of ways, from vocabulary lists to questions about current events. Basic background in some field of work, such as sociology or economics, may be sampled in a group of questions. Often these are principles which have become familiar to most persons through exposure rather than through formal training. It is difficult to advise you how to study for these questions; being alert to the world around you is our best suggestion.

2) Verbal ability

An example of an ability needed in many positions is verbal or language ability. Verbal ability is, in brief, the ability to use and understand words. Vocabulary and grammar tests are typical measures of this ability. Reading comprehension or paragraph interpretation questions are common in many kinds of civil service tests. You are given a paragraph of written material and asked to find its central meaning.

3) Numerical ability

Number skills can be tested by the familiar arithmetic problem, by checking paired lists of numbers to see which are alike and which are different, or by interpreting charts and graphs. In the latter test, a graph may be printed in the test booklet which you are asked to use as the basis for answering questions.

4) Observation

A popular test for law-enforcement positions is the observation test. A picture is shown to you for several minutes, then taken away. Questions about the picture test your ability to observe both details and larger elements.

5) Following directions

In many positions in the public service, the employee must be able to carry out written instructions dependably and accurately. You may be given a chart with several columns, each column listing a variety of information. The questions require you to carry out directions involving the information given in the chart.

6) Skills and aptitudes

Performance tests effectively measure some manual skills and aptitudes. When the skill is one in which you are trained, such as typing or shorthand, you can practice. These tests are often very much like those given in business school or high school courses. For many of the other skills and aptitudes, however, no short-time preparation can be made. Skills and abilities natural to you or that you have developed throughout your lifetime are being tested.

Many of the general questions just described provide all the data needed to answer the questions and ask you to use your reasoning ability to find the answers. Your best preparation for these tests, as well as for tests of facts and ideas, is to be at your physical and mental best. You, no doubt, have your own methods of getting into an exam-taking mood and keeping "in shape." The next section lists some ideas on this subject.

IV. KINDS OF QUESTIONS

Only rarely is the "essay" question, which you answer in narrative form, used in civil service tests. Civil service tests are usually of the short-answer type. Full instructions for answering these questions will be given to you at the examination. But in case this is your first experience with short-answer questions and separate answer sheets, here is what you need to know:

1) Multiple-choice Questions

Most popular of the short-answer questions is the "multiple choice" or "best answer" question. It can be used, for example, to test for factual knowledge, ability to solve problems or judgment in meeting situations found at work.

A multiple-choice question is normally one of three types—

- It can begin with an incomplete statement followed by several possible endings. You are to find the one ending which *best* completes the statement, although some of the others may not be entirely wrong.
- It can also be a complete statement in the form of a question which is answered by choosing one of the statements listed.
- It can be in the form of a problem – again you select the best answer.

Here is an example of a multiple-choice question with a discussion which should give you some clues as to the method for choosing the right answer:

When an employee has a complaint about his assignment, the action which will *best* help him overcome his difficulty is to

A. discuss his difficulty with his coworkers
B. take the problem to the head of the organization
C. take the problem to the person who gave him the assignment
D. say nothing to anyone about his complaint

In answering this question, you should study each of the choices to find which is best. Consider choice "A" – Certainly an employee may discuss his complaint with fellow employees, but no change or improvement can result, and the complaint remains unresolved. Choice "B" is a poor choice since the head of the organization probably does not know what assignment you have been given, and taking your problem to him is known as "going over the head" of the supervisor. The supervisor, or person who made the assignment, is the person who can clarify it or correct any injustice. Choice "C" is, therefore, correct. To say nothing, as in choice "D," is unwise. Supervisors have and interest in knowing the problems employees are facing, and the employee is seeking a solution to his problem.

2) True/False Questions

The "true/false" or "right/wrong" form of question is sometimes used. Here a complete statement is given. Your job is to decide whether the statement is right or wrong.

SAMPLE: A roaming cell-phone call to a nearby city costs less than a non-roaming call to a distant city.

This statement is wrong, or false, since roaming calls are more expensive.

This is not a complete list of all possible question forms, although most of the others are variations of these common types. You will always get complete directions for answering questions. Be sure you understand *how* to mark your answers – ask questions until you do.

V. RECORDING YOUR ANSWERS

Computer terminals are used more and more today for many different kinds of exams.

For an examination with very few applicants, you may be told to record your answers in the test booklet itself. Separate answer sheets are much more common. If this separate answer sheet is to be scored by machine – and this is often the case – it is highly important that you mark your answers correctly in order to get credit.

An electronic scoring machine is often used in civil service offices because of the speed with which papers can be scored. Machine-scored answer sheets must be marked with a pencil, which will be given to you. This pencil has a high graphite content which responds to the electronic scoring machine. As a matter of fact, stray dots may register as answers, so do not let your pencil rest on the answer sheet while you are pondering the correct answer. Also, if your pencil lead breaks or is otherwise defective, ask for another.

Since the answer sheet will be dropped in a slot in the scoring machine, be careful not to bend the corners or get the paper crumpled.

The answer sheet normally has five vertical columns of numbers, with 30 numbers to a column. These numbers correspond to the question numbers in your test booklet. After each number, going across the page are four or five pairs of dotted lines. These short dotted lines have small letters or numbers above them. The first two pairs may also have a "T" or "F" above the letters. This indicates that the first two pairs only are to be used if the questions are of the true-false type. If the questions are multiple choice, disregard the "T" and "F" and pay attention only to the small letters or numbers.

Answer your questions in the manner of the sample that follows:

32. The largest city in the United States is
    - A. Washington, D.C.
    - B. New York City
    - C. Chicago
    - D. Detroit
    - E. San Francisco

1) Choose the answer you think is best. (New York City is the largest, so "B" is correct.)
2) Find the row of dotted lines numbered the same as the question you are answering. (Find row number 32)
3) Find the pair of dotted lines corresponding to the answer. (Find the pair of lines under the mark "B.")
4) Make a solid black mark between the dotted lines.

VI. BEFORE THE TEST

Common sense will help you find procedures to follow to get ready for an examination. Too many of us, however, overlook these sensible measures. Indeed, nervousness and fatigue have been found to be the most serious reasons why applicants fail to do their best on civil service tests. Here is a list of reminders:

- Begin your preparation early – Don't wait until the last minute to go scurrying around for books and materials or to find out what the position is all about.
- Prepare continuously – An hour a night for a week is better than an all-night cram session. This has been definitely established. What is more, a night a week for a month will return better dividends than crowding your study into a shorter period of time.
- Locate the place of the exam – You have been sent a notice telling you when and where to report for the examination. If the location is in a different town or otherwise unfamiliar to you, it would be well to inquire the best route and learn something about the building.
- Relax the night before the test – Allow your mind to rest. Do not study at all that night. Plan some mild recreation or diversion; then go to bed early and get a good night's sleep.
- Get up early enough to make a leisurely trip to the place for the test – This way unforeseen events, traffic snarls, unfamiliar buildings, etc. will not upset you.
- Dress comfortably – A written test is not a fashion show. You will be known by number and not by name, so wear something comfortable.
- Leave excess paraphernalia at home – Shopping bags and odd bundles will get in your way. You need bring only the items mentioned in the official notice you received; usually everything you need is provided. Do not bring reference books to the exam. They will only confuse those last minutes and be taken away from you when in the test room.
- Arrive somewhat ahead of time – If because of transportation schedules you must get there very early, bring a newspaper or magazine to take your mind off yourself while waiting.
- Locate the examination room – When you have found the proper room, you will be directed to the seat or part of the room where you will sit. Sometimes you are given a sheet of instructions to read while you are waiting. Do not fill out any forms until you are told to do so; just read them and be prepared.
- Relax and prepare to listen to the instructions
- If you have any physical problem that may keep you from doing your best, be sure to tell the test administrator. If you are sick or in poor health, you really cannot do your best on the exam. You can come back and take the test some other time.

VII. AT THE TEST

The day of the test is here and you have the test booklet in your hand. The temptation to get going is very strong. Caution! There is more to success than knowing the right answers. You must know how to identify your papers and understand variations in the type of short-answer question used in this particular examination. Follow these suggestions for maximum results from your efforts:

1) Cooperate with the monitor

The test administrator has a duty to create a situation in which you can be as much at ease as possible. He will give instructions, tell you when to begin, check to see that you are marking your answer sheet correctly, and so on. He is not there to guard you, although he will see that your competitors do not take unfair advantage. He wants to help you do your best.

2) Listen to all instructions

Don't jump the gun! Wait until you understand all directions. In most civil service tests you get more time than you need to answer the questions. So don't be in a hurry. Read each word of instructions until you clearly understand the meaning. Study the examples, listen to all announcements and follow directions. Ask questions if you do not understand what to do.

3) Identify your papers

Civil service exams are usually identified by number only. You will be assigned a number; you must not put your name on your test papers. Be sure to copy your number correctly. Since more than one exam may be given, copy your exact examination title.

4) Plan your time

Unless you are told that a test is a "speed" or "rate of work" test, speed itself is usually not important. Time enough to answer all the questions will be provided, but this does not mean that you have all day. An overall time limit has been set. Divide the total time (in minutes) by the number of questions to determine the approximate time you have for each question.

5) Do not linger over difficult questions

If you come across a difficult question, mark it with a paper clip (useful to have along) and come back to it when you have been through the booklet. One caution if you do this – be sure to skip a number on your answer sheet as well. Check often to be sure that you have not lost your place and that you are marking in the row numbered the same as the question you are answering.

6) Read the questions

Be sure you know what the question asks! Many capable people are unsuccessful because they failed to *read* the questions correctly.

7) Answer all questions

Unless you have been instructed that a penalty will be deducted for incorrect answers, it is better to guess than to omit a question.

8) Speed tests

It is often better NOT to guess on speed tests. It has been found that on timed tests people are tempted to spend the last few seconds before time is called in marking answers at random – without even reading them – in the hope of picking up a few extra points. To discourage this practice, the instructions may warn you that your score will be "corrected" for guessing. That is, a penalty will be applied. The incorrect answers will be deducted from the correct ones, or some other penalty formula will be used.

9) Review your answers

If you finish before time is called, go back to the questions you guessed or omitted to give them further thought. Review other answers if you have time.

10) Return your test materials

If you are ready to leave before others have finished or time is called, take ALL your materials to the monitor and leave quietly. Never take any test material with you. The monitor can discover whose papers are not complete, and taking a test booklet may be grounds for disqualification.

VIII. EXAMINATION TECHNIQUES

1) Read the general instructions carefully. These are usually printed on the first page of the exam booklet. As a rule, these instructions refer to the timing of the examination; the fact that you should not start work until the signal and must stop work at a signal, etc. If there are any *special* instructions, such as a choice of questions to be answered, make sure that you note this instruction carefully.

2) When you are ready to start work on the examination, that is as soon as the signal has been given, read the instructions to each question booklet, underline any key words or phrases, such as *least*, *best*, *outline*, *describe* and the like. In this way you will tend to answer as requested rather than discover on reviewing your paper that you *listed without describing*, that you selected the *worst* choice rather than the *best* choice, etc.

3) If the examination is of the objective or multiple-choice type – that is, each question will also give a series of possible answers: A, B, C or D, and you are called upon to select the best answer and write the letter next to that answer on your answer paper – it is advisable to start answering each question in turn. There may be anywhere from 50 to 100 such questions in the three or four hours allotted and you can see how much time would be taken if you read through all the questions before beginning to answer any. Furthermore, if you come across a question or group of questions which you know would be difficult to answer, it would undoubtedly affect your handling of all the other questions.

4) If the examination is of the essay type and contains but a few questions, it is a moot point as to whether you should read all the questions before starting to answer any one. Of course, if you are given a choice – say five out of seven and the like – then it is essential to read all the questions so you can eliminate the two that are most difficult. If, however, you are asked to answer all the questions, there may be danger in trying to answer the easiest one first because you may find that you will spend too much time on it. The best technique is to answer the first question, then proceed to the second, etc.

5) Time your answers. Before the exam begins, write down the time it started, then add the time allowed for the examination and write down the time it must be completed, then divide the time available somewhat as follows:

- If 3-1/2 hours are allowed, that would be 210 minutes. If you have 80 objective-type questions, that would be an average of 2-1/2 minutes per question. Allow yourself no more than 2 minutes per question, or a total of 160 minutes, which will permit about 50 minutes to review.
- If for the time allotment of 210 minutes there are 7 essay questions to answer, that would average about 30 minutes a question. Give yourself only 25 minutes per question so that you have about 35 minutes to review.

6) The most important instruction is to *read each question* and make sure you know what is wanted. The second most important instruction is to *time yourself properly* so that you answer every question. The third most important instruction is to *answer every question*. Guess if you have to but include something for each question. Remember that you will receive no credit for a blank and will probably receive some credit if you write something in answer to an essay question. If you guess a letter – say "B" for a multiple-choice question – you may have guessed right. If you leave a blank as an answer to a multiple-choice question, the examiners may respect your feelings but it will not add a point to your score. Some exams may penalize you for wrong answers, so in such cases *only*, you may not want to guess unless you have some basis for your answer.

7) Suggestions
   a. Objective-type questions
      1. Examine the question booklet for proper sequence of pages and questions
      2. Read all instructions carefully
      3. Skip any question which seems too difficult; return to it after all other questions have been answered
      4. Apportion your time properly; do not spend too much time on any single question or group of questions
      5. Note and underline key words – *all, most, fewest, least, best, worst, same, opposite,* etc.
      6. Pay particular attention to negatives
      7. Note unusual option, e.g., unduly long, short, complex, different or similar in content to the body of the question
      8. Observe the use of "hedging" words – *probably, may, most likely,* etc.
      9. Make sure that your answer is put next to the same number as the question
      10. Do not second-guess unless you have good reason to believe the second answer is definitely more correct
      11. Cross out original answer if you decide another answer is more accurate; do not erase until you are ready to hand your paper in
      12. Answer all questions; guess unless instructed otherwise
      13. Leave time for review

   b. Essay questions
      1. Read each question carefully
      2. Determine exactly what is wanted. Underline key words or phrases.
      3. Decide on outline or paragraph answer

4. Include many different points and elements unless asked to develop any one or two points or elements
5. Show impartiality by giving pros and cons unless directed to select one side only
6. Make and write down any assumptions you find necessary to answer the questions
7. Watch your English, grammar, punctuation and choice of words
8. Time your answers; don't crowd material

8) Answering the essay question

Most essay questions can be answered by framing the specific response around several key words or ideas. Here are a few such key words or ideas:

M's: manpower, materials, methods, money, management
P's: purpose, program, policy, plan, procedure, practice, problems, pitfalls, personnel, public relations

a. Six basic steps in handling problems:
   1. Preliminary plan and background development
   2. Collect information, data and facts
   3. Analyze and interpret information, data and facts
   4. Analyze and develop solutions as well as make recommendations
   5. Prepare report and sell recommendations
   6. Install recommendations and follow up effectiveness

b. Pitfalls to avoid
   1. *Taking things for granted* – A statement of the situation does not necessarily imply that each of the elements is necessarily true; for example, a complaint may be invalid and biased so that all that can be taken for granted is that a complaint has been registered
   2. *Considering only one side of a situation* – Wherever possible, indicate several alternatives and then point out the reasons you selected the best one
   3. *Failing to indicate follow up* – Whenever your answer indicates action on your part, make certain that you will take proper follow-up action to see how successful your recommendations, procedures or actions turn out to be
   4. *Taking too long in answering any single question* – Remember to time your answers properly

IX. AFTER THE TEST

Scoring procedures differ in detail among civil service jurisdictions although the general principles are the same. Whether the papers are hand-scored or graded by machine we have described, they are nearly always graded by number. That is, the person who marks the paper knows only the number – never the name – of the applicant. Not until all the papers have been graded will they be matched with names. If other tests, such as training and experience or oral interview ratings have been given, scores will be combined. Different parts of the examination usually have different weights. For example, the written test might count 60 percent of the final grade, and a rating of training and experience 40 percent. In many jurisdictions, veterans will have a certain number of points added to their grades.

After the final grade has been determined, the names are placed in grade order and an eligible list is established. There are various methods for resolving ties between those who get the same final grade – probably the most common is to place first the name of the person whose application was received first. Job offers are made from the eligible list in the order the names appear on it. You will be notified of your grade and your rank as soon as all these computations have been made. This will be done as rapidly as possible.

People who are found to meet the requirements in the announcement are called "eligibles." Their names are put on a list of eligible candidates. An eligible's chances of getting a job depend on how high he stands on this list and how fast agencies are filling jobs from the list.

When a job is to be filled from a list of eligibles, the agency asks for the names of people on the list of eligibles for that job. When the civil service commission receives this request, it sends to the agency the names of the three people highest on this list. Or, if the job to be filled has specialized requirements, the office sends the agency the names of the top three persons who meet these requirements from the general list.

The appointing officer makes a choice from among the three people whose names were sent to him. If the selected person accepts the appointment, the names of the others are put back on the list to be considered for future openings.

That is the rule in hiring from all kinds of eligible lists, whether they are for typist, carpenter, chemist, or something else. For every vacancy, the appointing officer has his choice of any one of the top three eligibles on the list. This explains why the person whose name is on top of the list sometimes does not get an appointment when some of the persons lower on the list do. If the appointing officer chooses the second or third eligible, the No. 1 eligible does not get a job at once, but stays on the list until he is appointed or the list is terminated.

X. HOW TO PASS THE INTERVIEW TEST

The examination for which you applied requires an oral interview test. You have already taken the written test and you are now being called for the interview test – the final part of the formal examination.

You may think that it is not possible to prepare for an interview test and that there are no procedures to follow during an interview. Our purpose is to point out some things you can do in advance that will help you and some good rules to follow and pitfalls to avoid while you are being interviewed.

What is an interview supposed to test?

The written examination is designed to test the technical knowledge and competence of the candidate; the oral is designed to evaluate intangible qualities, not readily measured otherwise, and to establish a list showing the relative fitness of each candidate – as measured against his competitors – for the position sought. Scoring is not on the basis of "right" and "wrong," but on a sliding scale of values ranging from "not passable" to "outstanding." As a matter of fact, it is possible to achieve a relatively low score without a single "incorrect" answer because of evident weakness in the qualities being measured.

Occasionally, an examination may consist entirely of an oral test – either an individual or a group oral. In such cases, information is sought concerning the technical knowledges and abilities of the candidate, since there has been no written examination for this purpose. More commonly, however, an oral test is used to supplement a written examination.

Who conducts interviews?

The composition of oral boards varies among different jurisdictions. In nearly all, a representative of the personnel department serves as chairman. One of the members of the board may be a representative of the department in which the candidate would work. In some cases, "outside experts" are used, and, frequently, a businessman or some other representative of the general public is asked to serve. Labor and management or other special groups may be represented. The aim is to secure the services of experts in the appropriate field.

However the board is composed, it is a good idea (and not at all improper or unethical) to ascertain in advance of the interview who the members are and what groups they represent. When you are introduced to them, you will have some idea of their backgrounds and interests, and at least you will not stutter and stammer over their names.

What should be done before the interview?

While knowledge about the board members is useful and takes some of the surprise element out of the interview, there is other preparation which is more substantive. It *is* possible to prepare for an oral interview – in several ways:

1) Keep a copy of your application and review it carefully before the interview

This may be the only document before the oral board, and the starting point of the interview. Know what education and experience you have listed there, and the sequence and dates of all of it. Sometimes the board will ask you to review the highlights of your experience for them; you should not have to hem and haw doing it.

2) Study the class specification and the examination announcement

Usually, the oral board has one or both of these to guide them. The qualities, characteristics or knowledges required by the position sought are stated in these documents. They offer valuable clues as to the nature of the oral interview. For example, if the job involves supervisory responsibilities, the announcement will usually indicate that knowledge of modern supervisory methods and the qualifications of the candidate as a supervisor will be tested. If so, you can expect such questions, frequently in the form of a hypothetical situation which you are expected to solve. NEVER go into an oral without knowledge of the duties and responsibilities of the job you seek.

3) Think through each qualification required

Try to visualize the kind of questions you would ask if you were a board member. How well could you answer them? Try especially to appraise your own knowledge and background in each area, *measured against the job sought*, and identify any areas in which you are weak. Be critical and realistic – do not flatter yourself.

4) Do some general reading in areas in which you feel you may be weak

For example, if the job involves supervision and your past experience has NOT, some general reading in supervisory methods and practices, particularly in the field of human relations, might be useful. Do NOT study agency procedures or detailed manuals. The oral board will be testing your understanding and capacity, not your memory.

5) Get a good night's sleep and watch your general health and mental attitude

You will want a clear head at the interview. Take care of a cold or any other minor ailment, and of course, no hangovers.

What should be done on the day of the interview?

Now comes the day of the interview itself. Give yourself plenty of time to get there. Plan to arrive somewhat ahead of the scheduled time, particularly if your appointment is in the fore part of the day. If a previous candidate fails to appear, the board might be ready for you a bit early. By early afternoon an oral board is almost invariably behind schedule if there are many candidates, and you may have to wait. Take along a book or magazine to read, or your application to review, but leave any extraneous material in the waiting room when you go in for your interview. In any event, relax and compose yourself.

The matter of dress is important. The board is forming impressions about you – from your experience, your manners, your attitude, and your appearance. Give your personal appearance careful attention. Dress your best, but not your flashiest. Choose conservative, appropriate clothing, and be sure it is immaculate. This is a business interview, and your appearance should indicate that you regard it as such. Besides, being well groomed and properly dressed will help boost your confidence.

Sooner or later, someone will call your name and escort you into the interview room. *This is it.* From here on you are on your own. It is too late for any more preparation. But remember, you asked for this opportunity to prove your fitness, and you are here because your request was granted.

What happens when you go in?

The usual sequence of events will be as follows: The clerk (who is often the board stenographer) will introduce you to the chairman of the oral board, who will introduce you to the other members of the board. Acknowledge the introductions before you sit down. Do not be surprised if you find a microphone facing you or a stenotypist sitting by. Oral interviews are usually recorded in the event of an appeal or other review.

Usually the chairman of the board will open the interview by reviewing the highlights of your education and work experience from your application – primarily for the benefit of the other members of the board, as well as to get the material into the record. Do not interrupt or comment unless there is an error or significant misinterpretation; if that is the case, do not hesitate. But do not quibble about insignificant matters. Also, he will usually ask you some question about your education, experience or your present job – partly to get you to start talking and to establish the interviewing "rapport." He may start the actual questioning, or turn it over to one of the other members. Frequently, each member undertakes the questioning on a particular area, one in which he is perhaps most competent, so you can expect each member to participate in the examination. Because time is limited, you may also expect some rather abrupt switches in the direction the questioning takes, so do not be upset by it. Normally, a board member will not pursue a single line of questioning unless he discovers a particular strength or weakness.

After each member has participated, the chairman will usually ask whether any member has any further questions, then will ask you if you have anything you wish to add. Unless you are expecting this question, it may floor you. Worse, it may start you off on an extended, extemporaneous speech. The board is not usually seeking more information. The question is principally to offer you a last opportunity to present further qualifications or to indicate that you have nothing to add. So, if you feel that a significant qualification or characteristic has been overlooked, it is proper to point it out in a sentence or so. Do not compliment the board on the thoroughness of their examination – they have been sketchy, and you know it. If you wish, merely say, "No thank you, I have nothing further to add." This is a point where you can "talk yourself out" of a good impression or fail to present an important bit of information. Remember, *you close the interview yourself.*

The chairman will then say, "That is all, Mr. ______, thank you." Do not be startled; the interview is over, and quicker than you think. Thank him, gather your belongings and take your leave. Save your sigh of relief for the other side of the door.

How to put your best foot forward

Throughout this entire process, you may feel that the board individually and collectively is trying to pierce your defenses, seek out your hidden weaknesses and embarrass and confuse you. Actually, this is not true. They are obliged to make an appraisal of your qualifications for the job you are seeking, and they want to see you in your best light. Remember, they must interview all candidates and a non-cooperative candidate may become a failure in spite of their best efforts to bring out his qualifications. Here are 15 suggestions that will help you:

1) Be natural – Keep your attitude confident, not cocky

If you are not confident that you can do the job, do not expect the board to be. Do not apologize for your weaknesses, try to bring out your strong points. The board is interested in a positive, not negative, presentation. Cockiness will antagonize any board member and make him wonder if you are covering up a weakness by a false show of strength.

2) Get comfortable, but don't lounge or sprawl

Sit erectly but not stiffly. A careless posture may lead the board to conclude that you are careless in other things, or at least that you are not impressed by the importance of the occasion. Either conclusion is natural, even if incorrect. Do not fuss with your clothing, a pencil or an ashtray. Your hands may occasionally be useful to emphasize a point; do not let them become a point of distraction.

3) Do not wisecrack or make small talk

This is a serious situation, and your attitude should show that you consider it as such. Further, the time of the board is limited – they do not want to waste it, and neither should you.

4) Do not exaggerate your experience or abilities

In the first place, from information in the application or other interviews and sources, the board may know more about you than you think. Secondly, you probably will not get away with it. An experienced board is rather adept at spotting such a situation, so do not take the chance.

5) If you know a board member, do not make a point of it, yet do not hide it

Certainly you are not fooling him, and probably not the other members of the board. Do not try to take advantage of your acquaintanceship – it will probably do you little good.

6) Do not dominate the interview

Let the board do that. They will give you the clues – do not assume that you have to do all the talking. Realize that the board has a number of questions to ask you, and do not try to take up all the interview time by showing off your extensive knowledge of the answer to the first one.

7) Be attentive

You only have 20 minutes or so, and you should keep your attention at its sharpest throughout. When a member is addressing a problem or question to you, give him your undivided attention. Address your reply principally to him, but do not exclude the other board members.

8) Do not interrupt

A board member may be stating a problem for you to analyze. He will ask you a question when the time comes. Let him state the problem, and wait for the question.

9) Make sure you understand the question

Do not try to answer until you are sure what the question is. If it is not clear, restate it in your own words or ask the board member to clarify it for you. However, do not haggle about minor elements.

10) Reply promptly but not hastily

A common entry on oral board rating sheets is "candidate responded readily," or "candidate hesitated in replies." Respond as promptly and quickly as you can, but do not jump to a hasty, ill-considered answer.

11) Do not be peremptory in your answers

A brief answer is proper – but do not fire your answer back. That is a losing game from your point of view. The board member can probably ask questions much faster than you can answer them.

12) Do not try to create the answer you think the board member wants

He is interested in what kind of mind you have and how it works – not in playing games. Furthermore, he can usually spot this practice and will actually grade you down on it.

13) Do not switch sides in your reply merely to agree with a board member

Frequently, a member will take a contrary position merely to draw you out and to see if you are willing and able to defend your point of view. Do not start a debate, yet do not surrender a good position. If a position is worth taking, it is worth defending.

14) Do not be afraid to admit an error in judgment if you are shown to be wrong

The board knows that you are forced to reply without any opportunity for careful consideration. Your answer may be demonstrably wrong. If so, admit it and get on with the interview.

15) Do not dwell at length on your present job

The opening question may relate to your present assignment. Answer the question but do not go into an extended discussion. You are being examined for a *new* job, not your present one. As a matter of fact, try to phrase ALL your answers in terms of the job for which you are being examined.

Basis of Rating

Probably you will forget most of these "do's" and "don'ts" when you walk into the oral interview room. Even remembering them all will not ensure you a passing grade. Perhaps you did not have the qualifications in the first place. But remembering them will help you to put your best foot forward, without treading on the toes of the board members.

Rumor and popular opinion to the contrary notwithstanding, an oral board wants you to make the best appearance possible. They know you are under pressure – but they also want to see how you respond to it as a guide to what your reaction would be under the pressures of the job you seek. They will be influenced by the degree of poise you display, the personal traits you show and the manner in which you respond.

ABOUT THIS BOOK

This book contains tests divided into Examination Sections. Go through each test, answering every question in the margin. At the end of each test look at the answer key and check your answers. On the ones you got wrong, look at the right answer choice and learn. Do not fill in the answers first. Do not memorize the questions and answers, but understand the answer and principles involved. On your test, the questions will likely be different from the samples. Questions are changed and new ones added. If you understand these past questions you should have success with any changes that arise. Tests may consist of several types of questions. We have additional books on each subject should more study be advisable or necessary for you. Finally, the more you study, the better prepared you will be. This book is intended to be the last thing you study before you walk into the examination room. Prior study of relevant texts is also recommended. NLC publishes some of these in our Fundamental Series. Knowledge and good sense are important factors in passing your exam. Good luck also helps. So now study this Passbook, absorb the material contained within and take that knowledge into the examination. Then do your best to pass that exam.

———

EXAMINATION SECTION

EXAMINATION SECTION

TEST 1

DIRECTIONS: Each question or incomplete statement is followed by several suggested answers of completions. Select the one that BEST answers the question or completes the statement. *PRINT THE LETTER OF THE CORRECT ANSWER IN THE SPACE AT THE RIGHT.*

1. One of the major objectives of a pre-employment interview is to get the interviewee to respond freely to inquiries. The one of the following actions that would be *most likely* to restrict the conversation of the interviewee would be for the investigator to 1.______
   A. keep a stenographic record of the interviewee's statements
   B. ask questions requiring complete explanations
   C. pose direct, specific questions to the interviewee
   D. allow the interviewee to respond to questions at his own pace

2. *One* of the reasons for the widespread use of the interview in personnel selection is that the interview 2.______
   A. has been shown to be a valid measurement technique
   B. is efficient and reliable
   C. has been demonstrated to result in consistency among raters
   D. allows for flexibility of response

3. In conducting a personnel interview, which of the following guidelines would be MOST desirable for the interviewer to follow? 3.______
   A. Allocate the same amount of time to each person being interviewed to standardize the process.
   B. Ask exactly the same questions of all persons being interviewed to increase the objectivity of the process.
   C. Eliminate the use of non-directive techniques because of their subjectivity.
   D. Vary his style and technique to fit the purpose of the interview and the people being interviewed.

4. You are planning to conduct preliminary interviews of applicants for an important position in your department. Which of the following planning considerations is least *likely* to contribute to successful interviews? 4.______
   A. Make provisions to conduct interviews in privacy.
   B. Schedule your appointments so that interviews will be short.
   C. Prepare a list of your objectives.
   D. Learn as much as you can about the applicant before the interview.

5. When dealing with an aggrieved worker, a USEFUL interviewing technique is to 5.______
   A. maintain a sympathetic attitude
   B. maintain an attitude of cold impartiality
   C. assure the subject that you are on his side
   D. display a tape recorder to give the subject confidence that no parts of his story will be overlooked

6. The "patterned interview" is a device used by sophisticated employers to 6.______
   A. select employees who fit the ethnic pattern of the community
   B. ascertain the pattern of facts surrounding a grievance
   C. discourage workers from joining unions
   D. appraise a subject's most important character traits

7. One of the applicants for a menial job is a tall, stooped, husky individual with a low forehead, narrow eyes, a protruding chin, and a tendency to keep his mouth open. 7.______
   In interviewing him, you *should*
   A. check him more carefully than the other applicants regarding criminal background
   B. disregard any skills he might have for other jobs which are vacant
   C. make your vocabulary somewhat simpler than with the other applicants
   D. make no assumptions regarding his ability on the basis of his appearance

8. Of the following, the BEST approach for you to use at the beginning of an interview with a job applicant is to 8.______
   A. caution him to use his time economically and to get to the point
   B. ask him how long he intends to remain on the job if hired
   C. make some pleasant remarks to put him at ease
   D. emphasize the importance of the interview in obtaining the job

9. Of the following, the BEST reason for conducting an "exit interview" with an employee is to 9.______
   A. make certain that he returns all identification cards and office keys
   B. find out why he is leaving
   C. provide a useful training device for the exit interviewer
   D. discover if his initial hiring was in error

10. If you are to interview several applicants for jobs and rate them on five different factors on a scale of 1 to 5, you should be MOST careful to *insure* that your 10.______
    A. rating on one factor does not influence your rating on another factor
    B. ratings on all factors are interrelated with a minimum of variation
    C. overall evaluation for employment exactly reflects the arithmetic average of your ratings
    D. overall evaluation for employment is unrelated to your individual ratings

11. Of the following, the question MOST appropriate for initial screening purposes generally is: 11.______
    A. What are your salary requirements?
    B. Why do you think you would like this kind of work?
    C. How did you get along with your last supervisor?
    D. What are your vocational goals?

12: Of the following, *normally* the question MOST appropriate for selection purposes generally would tend to be: 12.______
    A. Where did you work last?
    B. When did you graduate from high. school?
    C. What was your average in school?
    D. Why did you select this organization?

13. Assume that you have been asked to interview each of several students who have been hired to work part-time. Which of the following would *ordinarily* be accomplished LEAST effectively in such-an interview? 13.______
   A. Providing information about the organization or institution in which the students will be Working.
   B. Directing the students to report for work each afternoon at specified times.
   C. Determining experience and background of the students so that appropriate assignments can be made.
   D. Changing the attitudes of the students toward the importance of parental controls.

14. In interviewing job applicants, which of the following usually does NOT have to be done before the end of the interview? 14.______
   A. Making a decision to hire an applicant.
   B. Securing information from applicants.
   C. Giving information to applicants.
   D. Establishing a friendly relationship with applicants.

15. In the process of interviewing applicants for a position on your staff, the *one* of the following which would be BEST is to 15.______
   A. make sure all applicants are introduced to the other members of your staff prior to the formal interview
   B. make sure the applicant does not ask questions about the job or the department
   C. avoid having the applicant talk with the staff under any circumstances
   D. introduce applicants to some of the staff at the conclusion of a successful interview

16. While interviewing a job applicant, you ask applicant left his last job. The applicant does not answer immediately. 16.______
   Of the following, the BEST action to take at that point is to
   A. wait until he answers
   B. ask another question
   C. repeat the question in a loud voice
   D. ask him why he does not answer

17. You know that a student applying for a job in your office has done well in college except for two courses in science. However, when you ask him about his grades, his reply is vague and general. 17.______
   It would be BEST for you to
   A. lead the applicant to admitting doing poorly in science to be sure that the facts are correct
   B. judge the applicant's tact and skill in handling what may be for him a personally sensitive question
   C. immediately confront the applicant with the facts and ask for an explanation
   D. ignore the applicant's response since you have the transcript

18. A college student has applied for a position with your department. Prior to conducting an interview of the job applicant, it would be LEAST helpful for you to have 18.______
   A. a personal resume
   B. a job description
   C. references
   D. hiring requirements

19. Job applicants tend to be nervous during interviews. Which of the following techniques is *most likely* to put such an applicant at ease? 19.______
    A. Try to establish rapport by asking general questions which are easily answered by the applicant.
    B. Ask the applicant to describe his career objectives immediately, thus minimizing the anxiety caused by waiting.
    C. Start the interview with another member of the' staff present so that the applicant does not feel alone.
    D. Proceed as rapidly as possible, since the emotional state of the applicant is none of your concern.

20. At the first interview between a supervisor and a newly appointed subordinate, GREATEST care should be taken to 20.______
    A. build toward a satisfactory personal relationship even if some other objectives of the interview must be postponed
    B. cover a predetermined list of specific objectives so as to make a further orientation interview unnecessary
    C. create an image of a forceful, determined supervisor whose wishes cannot be opposed by a subordinate without great risk
    D. create an impression of efficiency and control of operation free from interpersonal relationships

21. You are a supervisor in an agency and are holding your first interview with a new employee. In this interview, you should strive MAINLY to 21.______
    A. show the new employee that you are an efficient and objective supervisor, with a completely impersonal attitude toward your subordinates
    B. complete the entire orientation process including the giving of detailed job-duty instructions
    C. make it clear to the employee that all your decisions are based on your many years of experience
    D. lay the groundwork for a good employee-supervisor relationship by gaining the new employee's confidence

22. The INCORRECT statement related to the principles of interviewing is: 22.______
    A. Written outlines should be avoided by the interviewer because they tend to be overly restrictive.
    B. Preliminary planning (for the interview) should involve an analysis of the point of view of the person to be interviewed.
    C. An interviewing supervisor should make every effort to conduct it in privacy to avoid possible inhibitions.
    D. Well-planned questions are sometimes necessary in conducting an interview.

23. Assume that you are conducting an interview with a prospective employee who is of limited mental ability and low socio-economic status. Of the following, it is *most likely* that asking him many open-ended questions about his work experience would cause him to respond 23.______
    A. articulately
    B. reluctantly
    C. comfortably
    D. aggressively

24. An individual interview is to be used as part of an examination for a supervisory position. Of the following, the attribute or characteristic that is LEAST suitable for evaluation in such an, interview is 24.______
    A. ability to supervise people
    B. poise and confidence
    C. response to stress conditions
    D. rigidity and flexibility

25. In conducting a disciplinary interview, a supervisor finds that he must ask some highly personal questions which are relevant to the problem at hand. The interviewer is *most likely* to get TRUTHFUL answers to these questions if he asks them 25.______
    A. early in the interview, before the interviewee has had a chance to become emotional
    B. in a manner so that the interviewee can answer them with a simple "yes" or "no"
    C. well into the interview, after rapport and trust have been established
    D. just after the close of the interview, so that the questions appear to be off the record

---

KEY (CORRECT ANSWERS)

1. A
2. D
3. D
4. B
5. A
6. D
7. D
8. C
9. B
10. A
11. A
12. D
13. D
14. A
15. D
16. A
17. B
18. C
19. A
20. A
21. D
22. A
23. B
24. A
25. C

TEST 2

DIRECTIONS: Each question or incomplete statement is followed by several suggested answers of completions. Select the one that BEST answers the question or completes the statement. *PRINT THE LETTER OF THE CORRECT ANSWER IN THE SPACE AT THE RIGHT.*

1. Of the following methods of conducting an interview, the BEST is to 1.______
   A. ask questions with "yes" or "no" answers
   B. listen carefully and ask only questions that are pertinent
   C. fire questions at the interviewee so that he must answer sincerely and briefly
   D. read standardized questions to the person being interviewed

2. An interviewer should begin with topics which are easy to talk about and which are not threatening. 2.______
   This procedure is useful MAINLY because it
   A. allows the applicant a little time to get accustomed to the situation and leads to freer communication
   B. distracts the attention of the person being interviewed from the main purpose of the questioning
   C. is the best way for the interviewer to show that he is relaxed and confident on the job
   D. causes the interviewee to feel that the interviewer is apportioning valuable questioning time

3. The initial interview will normally be more of a problem to the interviewer than any subsequent interviews he may have with the same person because 3.______
   A. the interviewee is likely to be hostile
   B. there is too much to be accomplished in one session
   C. he has less information about the client than he will have later
   D. some information may be forgotten when later making record of this first interview

4. Most successful interviews are those in which the interviewer shows a genuine interest in the person he is questioning. 4.______
   This attitude would *most likely* cause the individual being interviewed to
   A. feel that the interviewer already knows all the facts in his case
   B. act more naturally and reveal more of his true feelings
   C. request that the interviewer give more attention to his problems, not his personality
   D. react defensively, suppress his negative feelings and conceal the real facts in his case

5. When interviewing a person, the interviewer may easily slip into error in rating his subject's personal qualities because of the general impression he receives of the individual. 5.______
   This tendency is known as the
   A. "halo" effect
   B. subjective bias problem
   C. "person-to-person" error
   D. inflation effect

6. An interviewer would find an interview check list LEAST useful for 6.______
   A. making sure that all the principal facts are secured in the interview
   B. insuring that the claimant's grievance is settled in his favor
   C. facilitating later research into the nature of the problems handled by the agency
   D. conducting the interview in a logical and orderly fashion

7. There are almost as many techniques of interviewing as there are interviewers. 7.______
   Of the following, the LEAST objectionable method is to
   A. ask if interviewee minds being quoted
   B. make occasional notes as important topics come up
   C. take notes unobtrusively
   D. take shorthand notes of every word

8. Questions worded so that the person being interviewed has some hint of the desired answer can modify the person's response. The result of the inclusion of such questions in an interview, even when they are used inadvertently, is to 8.______
   A. have no effect on the basic content of the information given by the person interviewed
   B. have value in convincing the person that the suggested plan is the best for him
   C. cause the person to give more meaningful information
   D. reduce the validity of the meaningful information obtained from the person

9. The person MOST likely to be a good interviewer is one who 9.______
   A. is able to outguess the person being interviewed
   B. tries to change the attitudes of the persons he interviews
   C. controls the interview by skillfully dominating the conversation
   D. is able to imagine himself in the position of the person being interviewed

10. The "halo effect" is an overall impression on the interviewee, whether favorable or unfavorable, usually created by a single trait. This impression then influences the appraisal of all other factors. A "halo effect" is *least likely* to be created at an interview where the interviewee is a 10.______
    A. person of average appearance and ability
    B. rough-looking man who uses abusive language
    C. young attractive woman being interviewed by a man
    D. person who demonstrates an exceptional ability to remember faces

11. Of the following, the BEST way for an interviewer to calm a person who seems to have become emotionally upset as a result of a question asked is for the interviewer to 11.______
    A. talk to the person about other things for a short time
    B. ask that the person control himself
    C. probe for the cause of his emotional upset
    D. finish the questioning as quickly as possible

12. Of the following, the GREATEST pitfall in interviewing is that the result may be affected by the 12.______
    A. bias of the interviewee
    B. bias of the interviewer
    C. educational level of the interviewee
    D. educational level of the interviewer

13. Assume you are assigned to interview applicants. 13.______
Of the following, which is the BEST attitude for you to take in dealing with applicants?
    A. Assume they will enjoy being interviewed because they believe that you have the power of decision
    B. Expect that they have a history of anti-social behavior in the family, and probe deeply into the social development of family members
    C. Expect that they will try to control the interview, thus you should keep them on the defensive
    D. Assume that they will be polite and cooperative and attempt to secure the information you need in a business-like manner

14. A Spanish-speaking applicant may want to bring his bilingual child with him to an interview to act as an interpreter. 'Which of the following would be LEAST likely to affect the value of an interview in which an applicant's child has acted as interpreter? 14.______
    A. It may make it undesirable to ask certain questions.
    B. A child may do an inadequate job of interpretation.
    C. A child's answers may indicate his feelings toward his parents.
    D. The applicant may not want to reveal all information in front of his child.

15. In answering questions asked by students, faculty, and the public, it is MOST important that 15.______
    A. you indicate your source of information
    B. you are not held responsible for the answers
    C. the facts you give be accurate
    D. the answers cover every possible aspect of each question

16. Assume that someone you are interviewing is reluctant to give you certain information. He would *probably* be MORE responsive if you show him that 16.______
    A. all the other persons you interviewed provided you with the information
    B. it would serve his own best interests to give you the information
    C. the information is very important to you
    D. you are business like and take a no-nonsense approach

17. Taking notes while you are interviewing someone is *most likely* to 17.______
    A. arouse doubts as to your trustworthiness
    B. give the interviewee confidence in your ability
    C. insure that you record the facts you think are important
    D. make the responses of the interviewee unreliable

18. In developing a role playing situation to be used to train interviewers, the one of the following that it would be MOST IMPORTANT to use as a guide is that the situation 18.______
    A. allow the role player to identify readily with the role he is to play
    B. be free of actual or potential conflict between the role players
    C. can be clearly recognized by the participants as an actual interview situation that has already taken place
    D. should provide a detailed set of specifications for handling the roles to be played

19. Restating a question before the person being interviewed gives an answer to the original question is usually NOT good practice *principally* because 19.______
    A. the client will think that you don't know your job
    B. it may confuse the client
    C. the interviewer should know exactly what to ask and how to put the question
    D. it reveals the interviewer's insecurity

20. In interviewing a man who has a grievance, it is IMPORTANT that the interviewer 20.______
    A. take note of such physical responses as shifty eyes
    B. use a lie detector, if possible, to ascertain the truth in doubtful situations
    C. allow the complainant to "tell his story"
    D. place the complainant under oath

21. Ideally, the setting for an interview should NOT include 21.____
    A. an informal opening
    B. privacy and comfort
    C. an atmosphere of leisure
    D. a lie detector

22. Which of the following is an example of a "non-directive" interview? 22.______
    A. The subject directs his remarks at someone other than the interviewer.
    B. The subject discusses any topics that seem to be relevant to him.
    C. The subject has not been directed that he need answer any particular questions.
    D. The interview is confined to the facts of the case and is not directed at eliciting personal information.

23. Of the following abilities, the one which is LEAST important in conducting an interview is the ability to 23.______
    A. ask the interviewee pertinent questions
    B. evaluate the interviewee on the basis of appearance
    C. evaluate the responses of the interviewee
    D. gain the cooperation of the interviewee

24. Which of the following actions would be LEAST desirable for you to take when you have to conduct an interview? 24.______
    A. Set a relaxed and friendly atmosphere.
    B. Plan you interview ahead of time.
    C. Allow the person interviewed to structure the interview as he wishes.
    D. Include some stock or standard question which you ask everyone.

25. One of the MOST important techniques for conducting good interviews is 25.______
    A. asking the applicant questions in rapid succession, thereby keeping the conversation properly focused
    B. listening carefully to all that the applicant has to say, making mental notes of possible areas for follow-up
    C. indicating to the applicant the criteria and standards on which you will base your judgment
    D. making sure that you are interrupted about five minutes before you wish to end so that you can keep on schedule

KEY (CORRECT ANSWERS)

1. B
2. A
3. C
4. B
5. A
6. B
7. C
8. D
9. D
10. A
11. A
12. B
13. D
14. C
15. C
16. B
17. C
18. A
19. B
20. C
21. D
22. B
23. B
24. C
25. B

INTERVIEWING
EXAMINATION SECTION
TEST 1

DIRECTIONS : Each question or incomplete statement is followed by several suggested answers or completions. Select the one that BEST answers the question or completes the statement. *PRINT THE LETTER OF THE CORRECT ANSWER IN THE SPACE AT THE RIGHT.*

1. You are conducting an interview with a client who has been having some difficulties with one of her fellow-workers. The client walks on crutches. You tell the client that she probably finds it difficult to get along with her fellow-workers because of this handicap. To make such a statement would, *generally,* be 1.____

   A. *proper;* people are often prejudiced against persons with physical deformities
   B. *proper;* statements such as this indicate to the client that you are sympathetic toward her
   C. *improper;* this approach would not help the client solve her problem
   D. *improper;* you should have discussed this handicap in relation to the client's continued ability to continue in her job

2. The information which the interviewer plans to secure from an individual with whom he talks is determined MAINLY by the 2.____

   A. purpose of the interview and the functions of the agency
   B. state assistance laws and the desires of the individual
   C. privacy they have while talking and the willingness of the individual to give information
   D. emotional feelings of the individual seeking help and the interviewer's reactions to these feelings

3. *Generally,* the MOST effective of the following ways of dealing with a person being interviewed who frequently digresses from the subject under discussion or starts to ramble, is for the interviewer to 3.____

   A. tell the person that he, the interviewer, will have to terminate the interview unless the former sticks to the point
   B. increase the tempo of the interview
   C. demonstrate that he is a good listener and allow the person to continue in his own way
   D. inject questions which relate to the purpose of the interview

4. "Being a good listener" is an interviewing technique which, if applied properly, is *desirable* MOSTLY because it 4.____

   A. catches the client more easily in misrepresentations and lies
   B. conserves the energies of the interviewer
   C. encourages the client to talk about his personal affairs without restraint
   D. encourages the giving of information which is generally more reliable and complete

5. When questioning applicants for eligibility, it would be BEST to ask questions that are 5.____

A. *direct,* so that the applicant will realize that the interviewer knows what he is doing
B. *direct,* so that the information received will be as pertinent as possible
C. *indirect,* so that the applicant will not realize the purpose of the interview
D. *indirect,* so that you can trap the applicant into making admissions that he would not otherwise make

6. The CHIEF reason for conducting an interview with a new applicant in complete privacy is that the 6.____

A. interviewer will be better able to record the facts without any other worker reading his case notes
B. applicant will be impressed by the business-like atmosphere of the agency
C. interviewer will be able to devote more time to questioning the applicant without interruption
D. applicant will be more likely to speak frankly

7. When conducting an interview with a client who is upset because of an increase in rent, it would be BEST for the interviewer to 7.____

A. agree with the client that the agency was wrong in raising his rent, as a basis for further discussion
B. tell the client that unless he calms down the interview will be ended
C. prevent the client from becoming emotional
D. tell the client the reasons for the increase

8. At an interview to determine whether an applicant is eligible, the applicant gives information different from that which he submitted on his application. 8.____
The MOST advisable action to take is to

A. cross out the old information, enter the new information, and initial the entry
B. re-enter the old information on the application form and initial the entry
C. give the applicant another application form, have him fill it out correctly, and resume the interview
D. give the applicant another application form to fill out, and set a later date for another interview

9. After you have secured,in an interview, all the necessary information from an applicant, he shows no intention of leaving, but starts to tell you a long personal story. 9.____
Of the following, the MOST advisable action for you to take is to

A. explain to the applicant why personal stories are out of place in a business office
B. listen carefully to the story for whatever relevant information it may contain
C. interrupt him tactfully, thank him for the information he has already given, and terminate the interview
D. inform your supervisor that the time required for this interview will prevent you from completing the interviews scheduled for the day

10. In interviewing, the practice of anticipating an applicant's answers to questions is, *generally,* 10.____

A. *desirable* because it is effective and economical when it is necessary to interview large numbers of applicants
B. *desirable* because many applicants have language difficulties

C. *undesirable* because it is the inalienable right of every person to answer as he sees fit
D. *undesirable* because applicants may tend to agree with the answer proposed by the interviewer even when the answer is not entirely correct

11. A follow-up interview was arranged for an applicant in order that he might furnish certain requested evidence. At this follow-up interview, the applicant still fails to furnish the necessary evidence. 11.____
It would be MOST advisable for you to

A. advise the applicant that he is now considered ineligible
B. ask the applicant how soon he can get the necessary evidence and set a date for another interview
C. question the applicant carefully and thoroughly to determine if he has misrepresented or falsified any information
D. set a date for another interview and tell the applicant to get the necessary evidence by that time

12. When an initial interview is being conducted, one way of starting is to explain the purpose of the interview to the applicant. 12.____
The practice of starting the interview with such an explanation is, *generally,*

A. *desirable* because the applicant can then understand why the interview is necessary and what will be accomplished by it
B. *desirable* because it creates the rapport which is necessary to successful interviewing
C. *undesirable* because time will be saved by starting off directly with the questions which must be asked
D. *undesirable* because the interviewer should have the choice of starting an interview in any manner he prefers

13. Empathy can be defined as the ability of one individual to respond sensitively and imaginatively to another's feelings. 13.____
For an interviewer to be empathic during an interview is *usually*

A. *undesirable,* mainly because an interviewer should never be influenced by the feelings of the one being interviewed
B. *desirable,* mainly because an interview will not be productive unless the interviewer takes the side of the person interviewed
C. *undesirable,* mainly because empathy usually leads an interviewer to be biased in favor of the person being interviewed
D. *desirable,* mainly because this ability allows the interviewer to direct his questions more effectively to the person interviewed

14. Assume that you must interview several people who know each other. 14.____
To gather them all in one group and question them TOGETHER, is, *generally,*

A. *good practice,* since any inaccurate information offered by one person would be corrected by others in the group
B. *poor practice,* since people in a group rarely pay adequate attention to questions
C. *good practice,* since the interviewer will save much time and effort in this way
D. *poor practice,* since the presence of several people can inhibit an individual from speaking

15. An effective interviewer should know that the one of the following reasons which LEAST describes why there is a wide range of individual behavior in human relations is that 15.____

    A. socio-economic status influences human behavior
    B. physical characteristics do not influence human behavior
    C. education influences human behavior
    D. childhood experience influences human behavior

16. An interviewer encounters an uncooperative interviewee. Of the following, the FIRST thing the interviewer should do in such a situation is to 16.____

    A. try various appeals to win the interviewee over to a cooperative attitude
    B. try to ascertain the reason for non-cooperation
    C. promise the interviewee that all data will be kept confidential
    D. alter his interviewing technique with the uncooperative interviewee

17. You discover that an interviewee who was requested to bring with him specific documents for his initial employment interview has forgotten the documents. 17.____
    Of the following, the BEST course of action to take is to

    A. give the person a reasonable amount of time to furnish the documents
    B. tell the person you will let him know how much additional time he has
    C. mark the person disqualified for employment; he has failed to provide reasonably requested data on time
    D. mark the person provisionally qualified for employment; upon receipt of the documents he will be permanently qualified

18. In checking interviewees' work experience, you realize that the person whom you are to interview is only marginally fluent in English and has, therefore, requested permission to bring a translator with him. 18.____
    Of the following, the BEST course of action is to inform the interviewee that

    A. outside translators may not be used
    B. only city translators may be used
    C. state law requires fluency in English of all civil servants
    D. he may be assisted in the interview by his translator

19. Assume that, during the course of an interview, you are verbally attacked by the person being interviewed. 19.____
    Of the following, it would be MOST advisable to

    A. answer back in a matter-of-fact manner
    B. ask the person to apologize and discontinue the interview
    C. ignore the attack but adjourn the interview to another day
    D. use restraint and continue the interview

20. Assume that you find that the person you are interviewing has difficulty finishing his sentences and seems to be groping for words. 20.____
    In such a case, the BEST approach for you to take is to

    A. say what you think the person has in mind
    B. proceed patiently without calling attention to the problem
    C. ask the person why he finds it difficult to finish his sentences
    D. interrupt the interview until the person feels more relaxed

21. The one of the following which BEST describes the effect of the *sympathetic approach* in interviewing on the interviewee is that it will 21.____

A. have no discernible effect on the interviewee
B. calm the interviewee
C. lead the interviewee to underemphasize his problems
D. mislead the interviewee

22. The one of the following characteristics which is a PRIMARY requisite for a successful interview is 22.____

A. total *curiosity*
B. total *sympathy*
C. complete *attention*
D. complete *dedication*

23. Assume that you have been assigned to conduct a follow-up interview with a primary witness. 23.____
The one of the following which is MOST important in arranging such an interview is to

A. keep the witness cooperative
B. conduct the matter in secret
C. allow the witness to determine where and when the interview takes place
D. conduct the interview as soon as possible to insure a strong case

24. By examining a candidate's employment record, an interviewer can determine many things about the candidate. Of the following, the one which is LEAST apparent from an employment record is the candidate's 24.____

A. character
B. willingness to work
C. capacity to get along with co-workers
D. potential for advancing in civil service

25. Assume that you are conducting an interview in which the person being interviewed is using the interview as a forum for venting his anti-civil service feelings. 25.____
Of the following, the FIRST thing that you should do is to

A. agree with the person; perhaps that will shorten the outburst
B. respectfully disagree with the person; the decorum of the interview has already been disrupted
C. courteously and objectively direct the interview to the relevant issue
D. reschedule the interview to another mutually agreeable time

KEY (CORRECT ANSWERS)

1. C
2. A
3. D
4. D
5. B
6. D
7. D
8. A
9. C
10. D
11. B
12. A
13. D
14. D
15. B
16. B
17. A
18. D
19. D
20. B
21. C
22. C
23. A
24. D
25. C

TEST 2

DIRECTIONS: Each question or incomplete statement is followed by several suggested answers or completions. Select the one that BEST answers the question or completes the statement. *PRINT THE LETTER OF THE CORRECT ANSWER IN THE SPACE AT THE RIGHT.*

1. The pattern of an interview is LARGELY set by the 1.____

   A. person being interviewed
   B. person conducting the interview
   C. nature of the interview
   D. policy of the agency employing the interviewer

2. Assume that a person being interviewed, who had been talking freely, suddenly tries to change the subject. 2.____
   To a trained interviewer, this behavior would mean that the person *probably*

   A. knew very little about the subject
   B. realized that he was telling too much
   C. decided that his privacy was being violated
   D. realized that he was becoming confused

3. Assume that you receive a telephone call from an unknown individual requesting information about a person you are currently interviewing. 3.____
   In such a situation, the BEST course of action for you to take is to

   A. give him the information over the telephone
   B. tell him to write to your department for the information
   C. send him the information, retaining a copy for your files
   D. tell him to call back, giving you additional time to check into the matter

4. In an interview, assuming that the interviewer was using a *non-directive approach* in this interview, of the following, the interviewer's most effective response would be: 4.____

   A. "You know, you are building a bad record of tardiness."
   B. "Can you tell me more about this situation?"
   C. "What kind of person is your superior?"
   D. "Do you think you are acting fairly towards the agency by being late so often?"

5. In an interview, assuming that the interviewer was using a *directed approach* in this interview, of the following, the interviewer's response should be: 5.____

   A. "That doesn't seem like much of an excuse to me."
   B. "What do you mean by saying that you've lost interest?"
   C. "What problems are there with the supervision you are getting?"
   D. "How do you think your tardiness looks in your personnel record?"

Questions 6-8.

DIRECTIONS: Answer Questions 6 through 8 only on the basis of information given in the passage below.

.A personnel interviewer, selecting job applicants, may find that he reacts badly to some people even on first contact. This reaction cannot usually be explained by things that the interviewee has done or said. Most of us have had the experience of liking or disliking, of feeling comfortable or uncomfortable with people on first acquaintance, long before we have had a chance to make a conscious, rational decision about them. Often, too, our liking or disliking is transmitted to the other person by subtle processes such as gestures, posture, voice intonations, or choice of words. The point to be kept in mind in this: the relations between people are complex and occur at several levels, from the conscious to the unconscious. This is true whether the relationship is brief or long, formal or informal.

Some of the major dynamics of personality which operate on the unconscious level are projection, sublimation, rationalization, and repression. Encountering these for the first time, one is apt to think of them as representing pathological states. In the extreme, they undoubtedly are, but they exist so universally that we must consider them also to be parts of normal personality.

Without necessarily subscribing to any of the numerous theories of personality, it is possible to describe personality in terms of certain important aspects or elements. We are all aware of ourselves as thinking organisms.

This aspect of personality, the conscious part, is important for understanding human behavior, but it is not enough. Many find it hard to accept the notion that each person also has an unconscious. The existence of the unconscious is no longer a matter of debate. It is not possible to estimate at all precisely what proportion of our total psychological life is conscious, what proportion unconscious. Everyone who has studied the problem, however, agrees that consciousness is the smaller part of personality. Most of what we are and do is a result of unconscious processes. To ignore this is to risk mistakes.

6. The passage above suggests that an interviewer can be MOST effective if he 6._____

   A. learns how to determine other peoples' unconscious motivations
   B. learns how to repress his own unconsciously motivated mannerisms and behavior
   C. can keep others from feeling that he either likes or dislikes them
   D. gains an understanding of how the unconscious operates in himself and in others

7. It may be inferred from the passage above that the "subtle processes, such as gestures, posture, voice intonation, or choice of words," referred to in the first paragraph, are, *usually,* 7._____

   A. in the complete control of an expert interviewer
   B. the determining factors in the friendships a person establishes
   C. controlled by a person's unconscious
   D. not capable of being consciously controlled

8. The passage above implies that various different personality theories are, *usually,* 8._____

   A. so numerous and different as to be valueless to an interviewer
   B. in basic agreement about the importance of the unconscious
   C. understood by the interviewer who strives to be effective
   D. in agreement that personality factors such as projection and repression are pathological

Questions 9-10.

DIRECTIONS: Answer Questions 9 and 10 ONLY on the basis of information given in the passage below.

Since we generally assure informants that what they say is confidential, we are not free to tell one informant what the other has told us. Even if the informant says, "I don't care who knows it; tell anybody you want to," we find it wise to treat the interview as confidential. An interviewer who relates to some informants what other informants have told him is likely to stir up anxiety and suspicion. Of course, the interviewer may be able to tell an informant what he has heard without revealing the source of his information. This may be perfectly appropriate where a story has wide currency so that an informant cannot infer the source of the information. But if an event is not widely known, the mere mention of it may reveal to one informant what another informant has said about the situation. How can the data be cross-checked in these circumstances?

9. The passage above implies that the anxiety and suspicion an interviewer may arouse by telling what.has been learned in other interviews is due to the 9.____

   A. lack of trust the person interviewed may have in the interviewer's honesty
   B. troublesome nature of the material which the interviewer has learned in other interviews
   C. fact that the person interviewed may not believe that permission was given to repeat the information
   D. fear of the person interviewed that what he is telling the interviewer will be repeated

10. The paragraph above is *most likely* part of a longer passage dealing with 10.____

    A. ways to verify data gathered in interviews
    B. the various anxieties a person being interviewed may feel
    C. the notion that people sometimes say things they do not mean
    D. ways an interviewer can avoid seeming suspicious

Questions 11-12.

DIRECTIONS: Answer Questions 11 and 12 ONLY on the basis of information given below.

The ability to interview rests not only on any single trait, but on a vast complex of them. Habits, skills, techniques, and attitudes are all involved. Competence in interviewing is acquired only after careful and diligent study, prolonged practice (preferably under supervision), and a good bit of trial and error; for interviewing is not an exact science, it is an art. Like many other arts, however, it can and must draw on science in several of its aspects.

There is always a place for individual initiative, for imaginative innovations, and for new combinations of old approaches. The skilled interviewer cannot be bound by a set of rules. Likewise, there is not a set of rules which can guarantee to the novice that his interviewing will be successful. There are, however, some accepted, general guide-posts which may help the beginner to avoid mistakes, learn how to conserve his efforts, and establish effective working relationships with interviewees; to accomplish, in short, what he set out to do.

11. According to the passage above, rules and standard techniques for interviewing are 11.____

A. helpful for the beginner, but useless for the experienced, innovative interviewer
B. destructive of the innovation and initiative needed for a good interviewer
C. useful for even the experienced interviewer, who may, however, sometimes go beyond them
D. the means by which nearly anybody can become an effective interviewer

12. According to the passage above, the one of the following which is a prerequisite to competent interviewing is 12.____

A. avoiding mistakes
B. study and practice
C. imaginative innovation
D. natural aptitude

Questions 13-16.

DIRECTIONS: Answer Questions 13 through 16 SOLELY on the basis of information given in the following paragraph.

The question of what material is relevant is not as simple as it might seem. Frequently material which seems irrelevant to the inexperienced has, because of the common tendency to disguise and distort and misplace one's feelings, considerable significance. It may be necessary to let the client "ramble on" for a while in order to clear the decks, as it were, so that he may get down to things that really are on his mind. On the other hand, with an already disturbed person, it may be important for the interviewer to know when to discourage further elaboration of upsetting material. This is especially the case where the worker would be unable to do anything about it. An inexperienced interviewer might, for instance, be intrigued with the bizarre elaboration of material that the psychotic produces, but further elaboration of this might encourage the client in his instability. A too random discussion may indicate that the interviewee is not certain in what areas the interviewer is prepared to help him, and he may be seeking some direction. Or again, satisfying though it may be for the interviewer to have the interviewee tell him intimate details, such revelations sometimes need to be checked or encouraged only in small doses. An interviewee who has "talked too much" often reveals subsequent anxiety. This is illustrated by the fact that? frequently after a "confessional" interview ,the interviewee surprises the interviewer by being withdrawn, inarticulate, or hostile, or by breaking the next appointment.

13. Sometimes a client may reveal certain personal information to an interviewer and subsequently, may feel anxious about this revelation. 13.____
If, during an interview, a client begins to discuss very personal matters, it would be BEST to

A. tell the client, in no uncertain terms, that you're not interested in personal details
B. ignore the client at this point
C. encourage the client to elaborate further on the details
D. inform the client that the information seems to be very personal

14. Clients with severe psychological disturbances pose an especially difficult problem for the inexperienced interviewer. 14.____
The difficulty lies in the possibility of the client's

A. becoming physically violent and harming the interviewer
B. "rambling on" for a while
C. revealing irrelevant details which may be followed by cancelled appointments
D. reverting to an unstable state as a result of interview material

15. An interviewer should be constantly alert to the possibility of obtaining clues from the client as to problem areas. 15.____
According to the above passage, a client who discusses topics at random may be

A. unsure of what problems the interviewer can provide help
B. reluctant to discuss intimate details
C. trying to impress the interviewer with his knowledge
D. deciding what relevant material to elaborate on

16. The evaluation of a client's responses may reveal substantial information that may aid the interviewer in assessing the problem areas that are of concern to the client. Responses that seemed irrelevant at the time of the interview may be of significance because 16.____

A. considerable significance is attached to all irrelevant material
B. emotional feelings are frequently masked
C. an initial "rambling on" is often a prelude to what -is actually bothering the client
D. disturbed clients often reveal subsequent anxiety

Questions 17-19.

DIRECTIONS: Answer Questions 17 through 19 SOLELY on the basis of the following paragraph.

The physical setting of the interview may determine its entire potentiality. Some degree of privacy and a comfortable relaxed atmosphere are important. The interviewee is not encouraged to give much more than his name and address if the interviewer seems busy with other things, if people are rushing about, if there are distracting noises. He has a right to feel that, whether the interview lasts five minutes or an hour, he has, for that time, the undivided attention of the interviewer. Interruptions, telephone calls, and so on, should be reduced to a minimum. If the interviewee has waited in a crowded room for what seems to him an interminably long period, he is naturally in no mood to sit down and discuss what is on his mind. Indeed, by that time the primary thing on his mind may be his irritation at being kept waiting, and he frequently feels it would be impolite to express this. If a wait or interruptions have been unavoidable, it is always helpful to give the client some recognition that these are disturbing and that he can naturally understand that they make it more difficult for him to proceed. At the same time if he protests that they have not troubled him, the interviewer can best accept his statements at their face value, as further insistence that they must have been disturbing may be interpreted by him as accusing, and he may conclude that the interviewer has been personally hurt by his irritation.

17. Distraction during an interview may tend to limit the client's responses. In a case where an interruption has occurred, it would be BEST for the interviewer to 17.____

A. terminate this interview and have it rescheduled for another time period
B. ignore the interruption since it is not continuous
C. express his understanding that the distraction can cause the client to feel disturbed
D. accept the client's protests that he has been troubled by the interruption

18. To maximize the rapport that can be established with the client, an appropriate physical setting is necessary. At the very least, some privacy would be necessary. *In addition,* the interviewer should 18.____

A. always appear to be busy in order to impress the client
B. focus his attention only on the client
C. accept all the client's statements as being valid
D. stress the importance of the interview to the client

19. Clients who have been waiting quite some time for their interview may, justifiably, become upset. However, a client *may initially* attempt to mask these feelings because he may 19.____

A. personally hurt the interviewer
B. want to be civil
C. feel that the wait was unavoidable
D. fear the consequences of his statement

20. You have been assigned to interview W, a witness, concerning a minor automobile accident. Although you have made no breach of the basic rules of contact and approach, you, nevertheless, recognize that you and W have a personality clash and that a natural animosity has resulted. Of the following, you MOST appropriately should 20.____

A. discuss the personality problem with W and attempt to resolve the difference
B. stop the interview on some pretext and leave in a calm and pleasant manner, allowing an associate to continue the interview
C. ignore the personality problem and continue as though nothing had happened
D. change the subject matter being discussed since the facts sought may be the source of the animosity

21. Assume that you desire to interview W, a reluctant witness to an event that took place several weeks previously. Assume further that the interview can take place at a location to be designated by the interviewer. Of the following, the place of interview should *preferably* be the 21.____

A. office of the interviewer
B. home of W
C. office of W
D. scene where the event took place

22. Assume that you are interviewing W, a witness. During the interview it becomes apparent that W's statements are inaccurate and at variance with the facts previously established. In these circumstances, it would be BEST for you to 22.____

A. tell W that his statements are inaccurate and point out how they conflict with previously established facts

B. reword your questions and ask additional questions about the facts being discussed
C. warn W that he may be required to testify under oath at a later date
D. ignore W's statements if you have other information that support the facts

23. Assume that W, a witness being interviewed by you, shows a tendency to ramble. His answers to your questions are lengthy and not responsive. 23.____
In this situation, the BEST action for you to take is to

A. permit W to continue because at some point he will tell you the information sought
B. tell W that he is rambling and unresponsive and that more will be accomplished if he is brief and to the point
C. control the interview so that complete and accurate information is obtained
D. patiently listen to W since rambling is W's style and it cannot be changed

24. Assume that you are interviewing a client. Of the following, the BEST procedure for you to follow in regard to the use of your notebook is to 24.____

A. take out your notebook at the start of the interview and immediately begin taking notes
B. memorize the important facts related during the interview and enter them after the interview has been completed
C. advise the client that all his answers are being taken down to insure that he will tell the truth
D. establish rapport with the client and ask permission to jot down various data in your notebook

25. In order to conduct an effective interview, an interviewer's attention must continuously be directed in two ways, toward himself as well as toward the interviewee. Of the following, the PRIMARY danger in this division of attention is that the 25.____

A. interviewer's behavior may become less natural and thus alienate the interviewee
B. interviewee's span of attention will be shortened
C. interviewer's response may be interpreted by the interviewee as being antagonistic
D. interviewee's more or less concealed prejudices will come to the surface

---

KEY (CORRECT ANSWERS)

1. B
2. B
3. B
4. B
5. C

6. D
7. C
8. B
9. D
10. A

11. C
12. B
13. D
14. D
15. A

16. B
17. C
18. B
19. B
20. B

21. A
22. B
23. C
24. D
25. A

READING COMPREHENSION
UNDERSTANDING AND INTERPRETING WRITTEN MATERIAL
EXAMINATION SECTION
TEST 1

DIRECTIONS: Each question or incomplete statement is followed by several suggested answers or completions. Select the one that BEST answers the question or completes the statement. *PRINT THE LETTER OF THE CORRECT ANSWER IN THE SPACE AT THE RIGHT.*

Questions 1-5.

DIRECTIONS: Questions 1 through 5 are to be answered SOLELY on the basis of the following passage.

The most effective control mechanism to prevent gross incompetence on the part of public employees is a good personnel program. The personnel officer in the line departments and the central personnel agency should exert positive leadership to raise levels of performance. Although the key factor is the quality of the personnel recruited, staff members other than personnel officers can make important contributions to efficiency. Administrative analysts, now employed in many agencies, make detailed studies of organization and procedures, with the purpose of eliminating delays, waste, and other inefficiencies. Efficiency is, however, more than a question of good organization and procedures; it is also the product of the attitudes and values of the public employees. Personal motivation can provide the will to be efficient. The best management studies will not result in substantial improvement of the performance of those employees who feel no great urge to work up to their abilities.

1. The above passage indicates that the KEY factor in preventing gross incompetence of public employees is the 1.____

   A. hiring of administrative analysts to assist personnel people
   B. utilization of effective management studies
   C. overlapping of responsibility
   D. quality of the employees hired

2. According to the above passage, the central personnel agency staff SHOULD 2.____

   A. work more closely with administrative analysts in the line departments than with personnel officers
   B. make a serious effort to avoid jurisdictional conflicts with personnel officers in line departments
   C. contribute to improving the quality of work of public employees
   D. engage in a comprehensive program to change the public's negative image of public employees

3. The above passage indicates that efficiency in an organization can BEST be brought about by 3.____

   A. eliminating ineffective control mechanisms
   B. instituting sound organizational procedures

C. promoting competent personnel
D. recruiting people with desire to do good work

4. According to the above passage, the purpose of administrative analysis in a public agency is to 4.____

A. prevent injustice to the public employee
B. promote the efficiency of the agency
C. protect the interests of the public
D. ensure the observance of procedural due process

5. The above passage implies that a considerable rise in the quality of work of public employees can be brought about by 5.____

A. encouraging positive employee attitudes toward work
B. controlling personnel officers who exceed their powers
C. creating warm personal associations among public employees in an agency
D. closing loopholes in personnel organization and procedures

Questions 6-8.

DIRECTIONS: Questions 6 through 8 are to be answered SOLELY on the basis of the following passage on Employee Needs.

EMPLOYEE NEEDS

The greatest waste in industry and in government may be that of human resources. This waste usually derives not from employees' unwillingness or inability, but from management's ineptness to meet the maintenance and motivational needs of employees. Maintenance needs refer to such needs as providing employees with safe places to work, written work rules, job security, adequate salary, employer-sponsored social activities, and with knowledge of their role in the overall framework of the organization. However, of greatest significance to employees are the motivational needs of job growth, achievement, responsibility, and recognition.

Although employee dissatisfaction may stem from either poor maintenance or poor motivation factors, the outward manifestation of the dissatisfaction may be very much alike, i.e., negativism, complaints, deterioration of performance, and so forth. The improvement in the lighting of an employee's work area or raising his level of pay won't do much good if the source of the dissatisfaction is the absence of a meaningful assignment. By the same token, if an employee is dissatisfied with what he considers inequitable pay, the introduction of additional challenge in his work may simply make matters worse.

It is relatively easy for an employee to express frustration by complaining about pay, washroom conditions, fringe benefits, and so forth; but most people cannot easily express resentment in terms of the more abstract concepts concerning job growth, responsibility, and achievement.

It would be wrong to assume that there is no interaction between maintenance and motivational needs of employees. For example, conditions of high motivation often overshadow poor maintenance conditions. If an organization is in a period of strong growth and expansion, opportunities for job growth, responsibility, recognition, and achievement are usually abundant, but the rapid growth may have outrun the upkeep of maintenance factors. In this situation, motivation may be high, but only if employees recognize the poor maintenance conditions as unavoidable and temporary. The subordination of maintenance factors cannot go on indefinitely, even with the highest motivation.

Both maintenance and motivation factors influence the behavior of all employees, but employees are not identical and, furthermore, the needs of any individual do not remain constant. However, a broad distinction can be made between employees who have a basic orientation toward maintenance factors and those with greater sensitivity toward motivation factors.

A highly maintenance-oriented individual, preoccupied with the factors peripheral to his job rather than the job itself, is more concerned with comfort than challenge. He does not get deeply involved with his work but does with the condition of his work area, toilet facilities, and his time for going to lunch. By contrast, a strongly motivation-oriented employee is usually relatively indifferent to his surroundings and is caught up in the pursuit of work goals.

Fortunately, there are few people who are either exclusively maintenance-oriented or purely motivation-oriented. The former would be deadwood in an organization, while the latter might trample on those around him in his pursuit to achieve his goals.

6. With respect to employee motivational and maintenance needs, the management policies of an organization which is growing rapidly will probably result 6.____

   A. more in meeting motivational needs rather than maintenance needs
   B. more in meeting maintenance needs rather than motivational needs
   C. in meeting both of these needs equally
   D. in increased effort to define the motivational and maintenance needs of its employees

7. In accordance with the above passage, which of the following CANNOT be considered as an example of an employee maintenance need for railroad clerks? 7.____

   A. Providing more relief periods
   B. Providing fair salary increases at periodic intervals
   C. Increasing job responsibilities
   D. Increasing health insurance benefits

8. Most employees in an organization may be categorized as being interested in 8.____

   A. maintenance needs *only*
   B. motivational needs *only*
   C. both motivational and maintenance needs
   D. money only, to the exclusion of all other needs

Questions 9-11.

DIRECTIONS: Questions 9 through 11 are to be answered SOLELY on the basis of the following passage on Good Employee Practices.

GOOD EMPLOYEE PRACTICES

As a city employee, you will be expected to take an interest in your work and perform the duties of your job to the best of your ability and in a spirit of cooperation. Nothing shows an interest in your work more than coming to work on time, not only at the start of the day but also when returning from lunch. If it is necessary for you to keep a personal appointment at lunch hour which might cause a delay in getting back to work on time, you should explain the situation to your supervisor and get his approval to come back a little late before you leave for lunch.

You should do everything that is asked of you willingly and consider important even the small jobs that your supervisor gives you. Although these jobs may seem unimportant, if you forget to do them or if you don't do them right, trouble may develop later.

Getting along well with your fellow workers will add much to the enjoyment of your work. You should respect your fellow workers and try to see their side when a disagreement arises. The better you get along with your fellow workers and your supervisor, the better you will like your job and the better you will be able to do it.

9. According to the above passage, in your job as a city employee, you are expected to 9.____

   A. show a willingness to cooperate on the job
   B. get your supervisor's approval before keeping any personal appointments at lunch hour
   C. avoid doing small jobs that seem unimportant
   D. do the easier jobs at the start of the day and the more difficult ones later on

10. According to the above passage, getting to work on time shows that you 10.____

   A. need the job
   B. have an interest in your work
   C. get along well with your fellow workers
   D. like your supervisor

11. According to the above passage, the one of the following statements that is NOT true is 11.____

   A. if you do a small job wrong, trouble may develop
   B. you should respect your fellow workers
   C. if you disagree with a fellow worker, you should try to see his side of the story
   D. the less you get along with your supervisor, the better you will be able to do your job

Questions 12-15.

DIRECTIONS: Questions 12 through 15 are to be answered SOLELY on the basis of the following passage on Employee Suggestions.

EMPLOYEE SUGGESTIONS

To increase the effectiveness of the city government, the city asks its employees to offer suggestions when they feel an improvement could be made in some government operation. The Employees' Suggestions Program was started to encourage city employees to do this.

Through this Program, which is only for city employees, cash awards may be given to those whose suggestions are submitted and approved. Suggestions are looked for not only from supervisors but from all city employees as any city employee may get an idea which might be approved and contribute greatly to the solution of some problem of city government

Therefore, all suggestions for improvement are welcome, whether they be suggestions on how to improve working conditions, or on how to increase the speed with which work is done, or on how to reduce or eliminate such things as waste, time losses, accidents or fire hazards. There are, however, a few types of suggestions for which cash awards cannot be given. An example of this type would be a suggestion to increase salaries or a suggestion to change the regulations about annual leave or about sick leave. The number of suggestions sent in has increased sharply during the past few years. It is hoped that it will keep increasing in the future in order to meet the city's needs for more ideas for improved ways of doing things.

12. According to the above passage, the MAIN reason why the city asks its employees for suggestions about government operations is to 12.____

    A. increase the effectiveness of the city government
    B. show that the Employees' Suggestion Program is working well
    C. show that everybody helps run the city government
    D. have the employee win a prize

13. According to the above passage, the Employees' Suggestion Program can approve awards ONLY for those suggestions that come from 13.____

    A. city employees
    B. city employees who are supervisors
    C. city employees who are not supervisors
    D. experienced employees of the city

14. According to the above passage, a cash award cannot be given through the Employees' Suggestion Program for a suggestion about 14.____

    A. getting work done faster
    B. helping prevent accidents on the job
    C. increasing the amount of annual leave for city employees
    D. reducing the chance of fire where city employees work

15. According to the above passage, the suggestions sent in during the past few years have 15.____

    A. all been approved
    B. generally been well written
    C. been mostly about reducing or eliminating waste
    D. been greater in number than before

Questions 16-18.

DIRECTIONS: Questions 16 through 18 are to be answered SOLELY on the basis of the following passage.

The supervisor will gain the respect of the members of his staff and increase his influence over them by controlling his temper and avoiding criticizing anyone publicly. When a mistake is made, the good supervisor will talk it over with the employee quietly and privately. The supervisor will listen to the employee's story, suggest the better way of doing the job, and offer help so the mistake won't happen again. Before closing the discussion, the supervisor should try to find something good to say about other parts of the employee's work. Some praise and appreciation, along with instruction, is more likely to encourage an employee to improve in those areas where he is weakest.

16. A good title that would show the meaning of the above passage would be 16.____

A. HOW TO CORRECT EMPLOYEE ERRORS
B. HOW TO PRAISE EMPLOYEES
C. MISTAKES ARE PREVENTABLE
D. THE WEAK EMPLOYEE

17. According to the above passage, the work of an employee who has made a mistake is more likely to improve if the supervisor 17.____

A. avoids criticizing him
B. gives him a chance to suggest a better way of doing the work
C. listens to the employee's excuses to see if he is right
D. praises good work at the same time he corrects the mistake

18. According to the above passage, when a supervisor needs to correct an employee's mistake, it is important that he 18.____

A. allow some time to go by after the mistake is made
B. do so when other employees are not present
C. show his influence with his tone of voice
D. tell other employees to avoid the same mistake

Questions 19-23.

DIRECTIONS: Questions 19 through 23 are to be answered SOLELY on the basis of the following passage.

In studying the relationships of people to the organizational structure, it is absolutely necessary to identify and recognize the informal organizational structure. These relationships are necessary when coordination of a plan is attempted. They may be with *the boss,* line supervisors, staff personnel, or other representatives of the formal organization's hierarchy, and they may include the *liaison men* who serve as the leaders of the informal organization. An acquaintanceship with the people serving in these roles in the organization, and its formal counterpart, permits a supervisor to recognize sensitive areas in which it is simple to get a conflict reaction. Avoidance of such areas, plus conscious efforts to inform other people of his own objectives for various plans, will usually enlist their aid and support. Planning *without people* can lead to disaster because the individuals who must act together to make any plan a success are more important than the plans themselves.

19. Of the following titles, the one that MOST clearly describes the above passage is 19.____

A. COORDINATION OF A FUNCTION
B. AVOIDANCE OF CONFLICT
C. PLANNING WITH PEOPLE
D. PLANNING OBJECTIVES

20. According to the above passage, attempts at coordinating plans may fail unless 20.____

A. the plan's objectives are clearly set forth
B. conflict between groups is resolved
C. the plans themselves are worthwhile
D. informal relationships are recognized

21. According to the above passage, conflict 21.____

A. may, in some cases, be desirable to secure results
B. produces more heat than light
C. should be avoided at all costs
D. possibilities can be predicted by a sensitive supervisor

22. The above passage implies that 22.____

A. informal relationships are more important than formal structure
B. the weakness of a formal structure depends upon informal relationships
C. liaison men are the key people to consult when taking formal and informal structures into account
D. individuals in a group are at least as important as the plans for the group

23. The above passage suggests that 23.____

A. some planning can be disastrous
B. certain people in sensitive areas should be avoided
C. the supervisor should discourage acquaintanceships in the organization
D. organizational relationships should be consciously limited

Questions 24-25.

DIRECTIONS: Questions 24 and 25 are to be answered SOLELY on the basis of the following passage.

Good personnel relations of an organization depend upon mutual confidence, trust, and good will. The basis of confidence is understanding. Most troubles start with people who do not understand each other. When the organization's intentions or motives are misunderstood, or when reasons for actions, practices, or policies are misconstrued, complete cooperation from individuals is not forthcoming. If management expects full cooperation from employees, it has a responsibility of sharing with them the information which is the foundation of proper understanding, confidence, and trust. Personnel management has long since outgrown the days when it was the vogue to *treat them rough and tell them nothing.* Up-to-date personnel management provides all possible information about the activities, aims, and purposes of the organization. It seems altogether creditable that a desire should exist among employees for such information which the best-intentioned executive might think would not interest them and which the worst-intentioned would think was none of their business.

24. The above passage implies that one of the causes of the difficulty which an organization might have with its personnel relations is that its employees 24.____

A. have not expressed interest in the activities, aims, and purposes of the organization
B. do not believe in the good faith of the organization

C. have not been able to give full cooperation to the organization
D. do not recommend improvements in the practices and policies of the organization

25. According to the above passage, in order for an organization to have good personnel relations, it is NOT essential that 25.____

A. employees have confidence in the organization
B. the purposes of the organization be understood by the employees
C. employees have a desire for information about the organization
D. information about the organization be communicated to employees

---

KEY (CORRECT ANSWERS)

1.	D	11.	D
2.	C	12.	A
3.	D	13.	A
4.	B	14.	C
5.	A	15.	D
6.	A	16.	A
7.	C	17.	D
8.	C	18.	B
9.	A	19.	C
10.	B	20.	D

21. D
22. D
23. A
24. B
25. C

TEST 2

Questions 1-8.

DIRECTIONS: Questions 1 through 8 are to be answered SOLELY on the basis of the following passage.

Important figures in education and in public affairs have recommended development of a private organization sponsored in part by various private foundations which would offer installment payment plans to full-time matriculated students in accredited colleges and universities in the United States and Canada. Contracts would be drawn to cover either tuition and fees, or tuition, fees, room and board in college facilities, from one year up to and including six years. A special charge, which would vary with the length of the contract, would be added to the gross repayable amount. This would be in addition to interest at a rate which would vary with the income of the parents. There would be a 3% annual interest charge for families with total income, before income taxes, of $50,000 or less. The rate would increase by 1/10 of 1% for every $1,000 of additional net income in excess of $50,000 up to a maximum of 10% interest. Contracts would carry an insurance provision on the life of the parent or guardian who signs the contract; all contracts must have the signature of a parent or guardian. Payment would be scheduled in equal monthly installments.

1. Which of the following students would be eligible for the payment plan described in the above passage? A 1.____

   A. matriculated student taking six semester hours toward a graduate degree
   B. matriculated student taking seventeen semester hours toward an undergraduate degree
   C. graduate matriculated at the University of Mexico taking eighteen semester hours toward a graduate degree
   D. student taking eighteen semester hours in a special pre-matriculation program

2. According to the above passage, the organization described would be sponsored in part by 2.____

   A. private foundations
   B. colleges and universities
   C. persons in the field of education
   D. persons in public life

3. Which of the following expenses could NOT be covered by a contract with the organization described in the above passage? 3.____

   A. Tuition amounting to $20,000 per year
   B. Registration and laboratory fees
   C. Meals at restaurants near the college
   D. Rent for an apartment in a college dormitory

4. The total amount to be paid would include ONLY the 4.____

   A. principal
   B. principal and interest
   C. principal, interest, and special charge
   D. principal, interest, special charge, and fee

5. The contract would carry insurance on the 5.____

A. life of the student
B. life of the student's parents
C. income of the parents of the student
D. life of the parent who signed the contract

6. The interest rate for an annual loan of $25,000 from the organization described in the above passage for a student whose family's net income was $55,000 should be 6.____

A. 3% B. 3.5% C. 4% D. 4.5%

7. The interest rate for an annual loan of $35,000 from the organization described in the above passage for a student whose family's net income was $100,000 should be 7.____

A. 5% B. 8% C. 9% D. 10%

8. John Lee has submitted an application for the installment payment plan described in the above passage. John's mother and father have a store which grossed $500,000 last year, but the income which the family received from the store was $90,000 before taxes. They also had $5,000 income from stock dividends. They paid $10,000 in income taxes. The amount of income upon which the interest should be based is 8.____

A. $85,000 B. $90,000 C. $95,000 D. $105,000

Questions 9-13.

DIRECTIONS: Questions 9 through 13 are to be answered SOLELY on the basis of the following passage.

Since an organization chart is pictorial in nature, there is a tendency for it to be drawn in an artistically balanced and appealing fashion, regardless of the realities of actual organizational structure. In addition to being subject to this distortion, there is the difficulty of communicating in any organization chart the relative importance or the relative size of various component parts of an organizational structure. Furthermore, because of the need for simplicity of design, an organization chart can never indicate the full extent of the interrelationships among the component parts of an organization.

These interrelationships are often just as vital as the specifications which an organization chart endeavors to indicate. Yet, if an organization chart were to be drawn with all the wide variety of criss-crossing communication and cooperation networks existent within a typical organization, the chart would probably be much more confusing than informative. It is also obvious that no organization chart as such can prove or disprove that the organizational structure it represents is effective in realizing the objectives of the organization. At best, an organization chart can only illustrate some of the various factors to be taken into consideration in understanding, devising, or altering organizational arrangements.

9. According to the above passage, an organization chart can be expected to portray the 9.____

A. structure of the organization along somewhat ideal lines
B. relative size of the organizational units quite accurately
C. channels of information distribution within the organization graphically
D. extent of the obligation of each unit to meet the organizational objectives

10. According to the above passage, those aspects of internal functioning which are NOT shown on an organization chart 10.____

    A. can be considered to have little practical application in the operations of the organization
    B. might well be considered to be as important as the structural relationships which a chart does present
    C. could be the cause of considerable confusion in the operations of an organization which is quite large
    D. would be most likely to provide the information needed to determine the overall effectiveness of an organization

11. In the above passage, the one of the following conditions which is NOT implied as being a defect of an organization chart is that an organization chart may 11.____

    A. present a picture of the organizational structure which is different from the structure that actually exists
    B. fail to indicate the comparative size of various organizational units
    C. be limited in its ability to convey some of the meaningful aspects of organizational relationships
    D. become less useful over a period of time during which the organizational facts which it illustrated have changed

12. The one of the following which is the MOST suitable title for the above passage is 12.____

    A. THE DESIGN AND CONSTRUCTION OF AN ORGANIZATION CHART
    B. THE INFORMAL ASPECTS OF AN ORGANIZATION CHART
    C. THE INHERENT DEFICIENCIES OF AN ORGANIZATION CHART
    D. THE UTILIZATION OF A TYPICAL ORGANIZATION CHART

13. It can be INFERRED from the above passage that the function of an organization chart is to 13.____

    A. contribute to the comprehension of the organization form and arrangements
    B. establish the capabilities of the organization to operate effectively
    C. provide a balanced picture of the operations of the organization
    D. eliminate the need for complexity in the organization's structure

Questions 14-16.

DIRECTIONS: Questions 14 through 16 are to be answered SOLELY on the basis of the following passage.

In dealing with visitors to the school office, the school secretary must use initiative, tact, and good judgment. All visitors should be greeted promptly and courteously. The nature of their business should be determined quickly and handled expeditiously. Frequently, the secretary should be able to handle requests, receipts, deliveries, or passes herself. Her judgment should determine when a visitor should see members of the staff or the principal. Serious problems or doubtful cases should be referred to a supervisor.

14. In general, visitors should be handled by the 14.____

A. school secretary
B. principal
C. appropriate supervisor
D. person who is free

15. It is wise to obtain the following information from visitors: 15.____

A. Name
B. Nature of business
C. Address
D. Problems they have

16. All visitors who wish to see members of the staff should 16.____

A. be permitted to do so
B. produce identification
C. do so for valid reasons only
D. be processed by a supervisor

Questions 17-19.

DIRECTIONS: Questions 17 through 19 are to be answered SOLELY on the basis of the following passage.

Information regarding payroll status, salary differentials, promotional salary increments, deductions, and pension payments should be given to all members of the staff who have questions regarding these items. On occasion, if the secretary is uncertain regarding the information, the staff member should be referred to the principal or the appropriate agency. No question by a staff member regarding payroll status should be brushed aside as immaterial or irrelevant. The school secretary must always try to handle the question or pass it on to the person who can handle it.

17. If a teacher is dissatisfied with information regarding her salary status, as given by the school secretary, the matter should be 17.____

A. dropped
B. passed on to the principal
C. passed on by the secretary to proper agency or the principal
D. made a basis for grievance procedures

18. The following is an adequate summary of the above passage: 18.____

A. The secretary must handle all payroll matters
B. The secretary must handle all payroll matters or know who can handle them
C. The secretary or the principal must handle all payroll matters
D. Payroll matters too difficult to handle must be followed up until they are solved

19. The above passage implies that 19.____

A. many teachers ask immaterial questions regarding payroll status
B. few teachers ask irrelevant pension questions
C. no teachers ask immaterial salary questions
D. no question regarding salary should be considered irrelevant

Questions 20-22.

DIRECTIONS: Questions 20 through 22 are to be answered SOLELY on the basis of the following passage.

The necessity for good speech on the part of the school secretary cannot be overstated. The school secretary must deal with the general public, the pupils, the members of the staff, and the school supervisors. In every situation which involves the general public, the secretary serves as a representative of the school. In dealing with pupils, the secretary's speech must serve as a model from which students may guide themselves. Slang, colloquialisms, malapropisms, and local dialects must be avoided.

20. The above passage implies that the speech pattern of the secretary must be 20.____

A. perfect
B. very good
C. average
D. on a level with that of the pupils

21. The last sentence indicates that slang 21.____

A. is acceptable
B. occurs in all speech
C. might be used occasionally
D. should be shunned

22. The above passage implies that the speech of pupils 22.____

A. may be influenced
B. does not change readily
C. is generally good
D. is generally poor

Questions 23-25.

DIRECTIONS: Questions 23 through 25 are to be answered SOLELY on the basis of the following passage.

The school secretary who is engaged in the task of filing records and correspondence should follow a general set of rules. Items which are filed should be available to other secretaries or to supervisors quickly and easily by means of the application of a modicum of common sense and good judgment. Items which, by their nature, may be difficult to find should be cross-indexed. Folders and drawers should be neatly and accurately labeled. There should never be a large accumulation of papers which have not been filed.

23. A good general rule to follow in filing is that materials should be 23.____

A. placed in folders quickly
B. neatly stored
C. readily available
D. cross-indexed

24. Items that are filed should be available to 24.____

A. the secretary charged with the task of filing
B. secretaries and supervisors
C. school personnel
D. the principal

25. A modicum of common sense means ______ common sense. 25.____

A. an average amount of
B. a great deal of
C. a little
D. no

KEY (CORRECT ANSWERS)

1. B
2. A
3. C
4. C
5. D
6. B
7. B
8. C
9. A
10. B
11. D
12. C
13. A
14. A
15. B
16. C
17. C
18. B
19. D
20. B
21. D
22. A
23. C
24. B
25. C

TEST 3

Questions 1-4.

DIRECTIONS: Questions 1 through 4 are to be answered SOLELY on the basis of the following passage.

The proposition that administrative activity is essentially the same in all organizations appears to underlie some of the practices in the administration of private higher education. Although the practice is unusual in public education, there are numerous instances of industrial, governmental, or military administrators being assigned to private institutions of higher education and, to a lesser extent, of college and university presidents assuming administrative positions in other types of organizations. To test this theory that administrators are interchangeable, there is a need for systematic observation and classification. The myth that an educational administrator must first have experience in the teaching profession is firmly rooted in a long tradition that has historical prestige. The myth is bound up in the expectations of the public and personnel surrounding the administrator. Since administrative success depends significantly on how well an administrator meets the expectations others have of him, the myth may be more powerful than the special experience in helping the administrator attain organizational and educational objectives. Educational administrators who have risen through the teaching profession have often expressed nostalgia for the life of a teacher or scholar, but there is no evidence that this nostalgia contributes to administrative success

1. Which of the following statements as completed is MOST consistent with the above passage? The greatest number of administrators has moved from 1._____

   A. industry and the military to government and universities
   B. government and universities to industry and the military
   C. government, the armed forces, and industry to colleges and universities
   D. colleges and universities to government, the armed forces, and industry

2. Of the following, the MOST reasonable inference from the above passage is that a specific area requiring further research is the 2._____

   A. place of myth in the tradition and history of the educational profession
   B. relative effectiveness of educational administrators from inside and outside the teaching profession
   C. performance of administrators in the administration of public colleges
   D. degree of reality behind the nostalgia for scholarly pursuits often expressed by educational administrators

3. According to the above passage, the value to an educational administrator of experience in the teaching profession 3._____

   A. lies in the firsthand knowledge he has acquired of immediate educational problems
   B. may lie in the belief of his colleagues, subordinates, and the public that such experience is necessary
   C. has been supported by evidence that the experience contributes to administrative success in educational fields
   D. would be greater if the administrator were able to free himself from nostalgia for his former duties

4. Of the following, the MOST suitable title for the above passage is 4.____

   A. EDUCATIONAL ADMINISTRATION, ITS PROBLEMS
   B. THE EXPERIENCE NEEDED FOR EDUCATIONAL ADMINISTRATION
   C. ADMINISTRATION IN HIGHER EDUCATION
   D. EVALUATING ADMINISTRATIVE EXPERIENCE

Questions 5-6.

DIRECTIONS: Questions 5 and 6 are to be answered SOLELY on the basis of the following passage.

Management by objectives (MBO) may be defined as the process by which the superior and the subordinate managers of an organization jointly define its common goals, define each individual's major areas of responsibility in terms of the results expected of him and use these measures as guides for operating the unit and assessing the contribution of each of its members.

The MBO approach requires that after organizational goals are established and communicated, targets must be set for each individual position which are congruent with organizational goals. Periodic performance reviews and a final review using the objectives set as criteria are also basic to this approach.

Recent studies have shown that MBO programs are influenced by attitudes and perceptions of the boss, the company, the reward-punishment system, and the program itself. In addition, the manner in which the MBO program is carried out can influence the success of the program. A study done in the late sixties indicates that the best results are obtained when the manager sets goals which deal with significant problem areas in the organizational unit, or with the subordinate's personal deficiencies. These goals must be clear with regard to what is expected of the subordinate. The frequency of feedback is also important in the success of a management-by-objectives program. Generally, the greater the amount of feedback, the more successful the MBO program.

5. According to the above passage, the expected output for individual employees should be determined 5.____

   A. after a number of reviews of work performance
   B. after common organizational goals are defined
   C. before common organizational goals are defined
   D. on the basis of an employee's personal qualities

6. According to the above passage, the management-by-objectives approach requires 6.____

   A. less feedback than other types of management programs
   B. little review of on-the-job performance after the initial setting of goals
   C. general conformance between individual goals and organizational goals
   D. the setting of goals which deal with minor problem areas in the organization

Questions 7-10.

DIRECTIONS: Questions 7 through 10 are to be answered SOLELY on the basis of the following passage.

Management, which is the function of executive leadership, has as its principal phases the planning, organizing, and controlling of the activities of subordinate groups in the accomplishment of organizational objectives. Planning specifies the kind and extent of the factors, forces, and effects, and the relationships among them, that will be required for satisfactory accomplishment. The nature of the objectives and their requirements must be known before determinations can be made as to what must be done, how it must be done and why, where actions should take place, who should be responsible, and similar problems pertaining to the formulation of a plan. Organizing, which creates the conditions that must be present before the execution of the plan can be undertaken successfully, cannot be done intelligently without knowledge of the organizational objectives. Control, which has to do with the constraint and regulation of activities entering into the execution of the plan, must be exercised in accordance with the characteristics and requirements of the activities demanded by the plan.

7. The one of the following which is the MOST suitable title for the above passage is 7.____

   A. THE NATURE OF SUCCESSFUL ORGANIZATION
   B. THE PLANNING OF MANAGEMENT FUNCTIONS
   C. THE IMPORTANCE OF ORGANIZATIONAL FUNCTIONS
   D. THE PRINCIPLE ASPECTS OF MANAGEMENT

8. It can be inferred from the above passage that the one of the following functions whose existence is essential to the existence of the other three is the 8.____

   A. regulation of the work needed to carry out a plan
   B. understanding of what the organization intends to accomplish
   C. securing of information of the factors necessary for accomplishment of objectives
   D. establishment of the conditions required for successful action

9. The one of the following which would NOT be included within any of the principal phases of the function of executive leadership as defined in the above passage is 9.____

   A. determination of manpower requirements
   B. procurement of required material
   C. establishment of organizational objectives
   D. scheduling of production

10. The conclusion which can MOST reasonably be drawn from the above passage is that the control phase of managing is most directly concerned with the 10.____

   A. influencing of policy determinations
   B. administering of suggestion systems
   C. acquisition of staff for the organization
   D. implementation of performance standards

Questions 11-12.

DIRECTIONS: Questions 11 and 12 are to be answered SOLELY on the basis of the following passage.

Under an open-and-above-board policy, it is to be expected that some supervisors will gloss over known shortcomings of subordinates rather than face the task of discussing them face-to-face. It is also to be expected that at least some employees whose job performance is below par will reject the supervisor's appraisal as biased and unfair. Be that as it may, these are inescapable aspects of any performance appraisal system in which human beings are involved. The supervisor who shies away from calling a spade a spade, as well as the employee with a chip on his shoulder, will each in his own way eventually be revealed in his true light--to the benefit of the organization as a whole.

11. The BEST of the following interpretations of the above passage is that 11._____

A. the method of rating employee performance requires immediate revision to improve employee acceptance
B. substandard performance ratings should be discussed with employees even if satisfactory ratings are not
C. supervisors run the risk of being called unfair by their subordinates even though their appraisals are accurate
D. any system of employee performance rating is satisfactory if used properly

12. The BEST of the following interpretations of the above passage is that 12._____

A. supervisors generally are not open-and-above-board with their subordinates
B. it is necessary for supervisors to tell employees objectively how they are performing
C. employees complain when their supervisor does not keep them informed
D. supervisors are afraid to tell subordinates their weaknesses

Questions 13-15.

DIRECTIONS: Questions 13 through 15 are to be answered SOLELY on the basis of the following passage.

During the last decade, a great deal of interest has been generated around the phenomenon of *organizational development,* or the process of developing human resources through conscious organization effort. Organizational development (OD) stresses improving interpersonal relationships and organizational skills, such as communication, to a much greater degree than individual training ever did. The kind of training that an organization should emphasize depends upon the present and future structure of the organization. If future organizations are to be unstable, shifting coalitions, then individual skills and abilities, particularly those emphasizing innovativeness, creativity, flexibility, and the latest technological knowledge, are crucial and individual training is most appropriate.

But if there is to be little change in organizational structure, then the main thrust of training should be group-oriented or organizational development. This approach seems better designed for overcoming hierarchical barriers, for developing a degree of interpersonal relationships which make communication along the chain of command possible, and for retaining a modicum of innovation and/or flexibility.

13. According to the above passage, group-oriented training is MOST useful in 13._____

A. developing a communications system that will facilitate understanding through the chain of command
B. highly flexible and mobile organizations
C. preventing the crossing of hierarchical barriers within an organization
D. saving energy otherwise wasted on developing methods of dealing with rigid hierarchies

14. The one of the following conclusions which can be drawn MOST appropriately from the above passage is that 14.____

A. behavioral research supports the use of organizational development training methods rather than individualized training
B. it is easier to provide individualized training in specific skills than to set up sensitivity training programs
C. organizational development eliminates innovative or flexible activity
D. the nature of an organization greatly influences which training methods will be most effective

15. According to the above passage, the one of the following which is LEAST important for large-scale organizations geared to rapid and abrupt change is 15.____

A. current technological information
B. development of a high degree of interpersonal relationships
C. development of individual skills and abilities
D. emphasis on creativity

Questions 16-18.

DIRECTIONS: Questions 16 through 18 are to be answered SOLELY on the basis of the following passage.

The increase in the extent to which each individual is personally responsible to others is most noticeable in a large bureaucracy. No one person *decides* anything; each decision of any importance, is the product of an intricate process of brokerage involving individuals inside and outside the organization who feel some reason to be affected by the decision, or who have special knowledge to contribute to it. The more varied the organization's constituency, the more outside *veto-groups* will need to be taken into account. But even if no outside consultations were involved, sheer size would produce a complex process of decision. For a large organization is a deliberately created system of tensions into which each individual is expected to bring work-ways, viewpoints, and outside relationships markedly different from those of his colleagues. It is the administrator's task to draw from these disparate forces the elements of wise action from day to day, consistent with the purposes of the organization as a whole.

16. The above passage is essentially a description of decision making as 16.____

A. an organization process
B. the key responsibility of the administrator
C. the one best position among many
D. a complex of individual decisions

17. Which one of the following statements BEST describes the responsibilities of an administrator? 17.____

A. He modifies decisions and goals in accordance with pressures from within and outside the organization.
B. He creates problem-solving mechanisms that rely on the varied interests of his staff and *veto-groups*.
C. He makes determinations that will lead to attainment of his agency's objectives.
D. He obtains agreement among varying viewpoints and interests.

18. In the context of the operations of a central public personnel agency, a *veto group* would LEAST likely consist of 18.____

A. employee organizations
B. professional personnel societies
C. using agencies
D. civil service newspapers

Questions 19-25.

DIRECTIONS: Questions 19 through 25 are to be answered SOLELY on the basis of the following passage, which is an extract from a report prepared for Department X, which outlines the procedure to be followed in the case of transfers of employees.

Every transfer, regardless of the reason therefore, requires completion of the record of transfer, Form DT 411. To denote consent to the transfer, DT 411 should contain the signatures of the transferee and the personnel officer(s) concerned, except that, in the case of an involuntary transfer, the signatures of the transferee's present and prospective supervisors shall be entered in Boxes 8A and 8B, respectively, since the transferee does not consent. Only a permanent employee may request a transfer; in such cases, the employee's attendance record shall be duly considered with regard to absences, latenesses, and accrued overtime balances. In the case of an inter-district transfer, the employee's attendance record must be included in Section 8A of the transfer request, Form DT 410, by the personnel officer of the district from which the transfer is requested. The personnel officer of the district to which the employee requested transfer may refuse to accept accrued overtime balances in excess of ten days.

An employee on probation shall be eligible for transfer. If such employee is involuntarily transferred, he shall be credited for the period of time already served on probation. However, if such transfer is voluntary, the employee shall be required to serve the entire period of his probation in the new position. An employee who has occurred a disability which prevents him from performing his normal duties may be transferred during the period of such disability to other appropriate duties. A disability transfer requires the completion of either Form DT 414 if the disability is job-connected, or Form DT 415 if it is not a job-connected disability. In either case, the personnel officer of the district from which the transfer is made signs in Box 6A of the first two copies and the personnel officer of the district to which the transfer is made signs in Box 6B of the last two copies, or, in the case of an intra-district disability transfer, the personnel officer must sign in Box 6A of the first two copies and Box 6B of the last two copies.

19. When a personnel officer consents to an employee's request for transfer from his district, this procedure requires that the personnel officer sign Form(s) 19.____

A. DT 411
B. DT 410 and DT 411
C. DT 411 and either Form DT 414 or DT 415
D. DT 410 and DT 411, and either Form DT 414 or DT 415

20. With respect to the time record of an employee transferred against his wishes during his probationary period, this procedure requires that 20.____

A. he serve the entire period of his probation in his present office
B. he lose his accrued overtime balance

C. his attendance record be considered with regard to absences and latenesses
D. he be given credit for the period of time he has already served on probation

21. Assume you are a supervisor and an employee must be transferred into your office against his wishes. According to the this procedure, the box you must sign on the record of transfer is 21.____

A. 6A B. 8A C. 6B D. 8B

22. Under this procedure, in the case of a disability transfer, when must Box 6A on Forms DT 414 and DT 415 be signed by the personnel officer of the district to which the transfer is being made? 22.____

A. In all cases when either Form DT 414 or Form DT 415 is used
B. In all cases when Form DT 414 is used and only under certain circumstances when Form DT 415 is used
C. In all cases when Form DT 415 is used and only under certain circumstances when Form DT 414 is used
D. Only under certain circumstances when either Form DT 414 or Form DT 415 is used

23. From the above passage, it may be inferred MOST correctly that the number of copies of Form DT 414 is 23.____

A. no more than 2
B. at least 3
C. at least 5
D. more than the number of copies of Form DT 415

24. A change in punctuation and capitalization only which would change one sentence into two and possibly contribute to somewhat greater ease of reading this report extract would be MOST appropriate in the 24.____

A. 2nd sentence, 1st paragraph
B. 3rd sentence, 1st paragraph
C. next to he last sentence, 2nd paragraph
D. 2nd sentence, 2nd paragraph

25. In the second paragraph, a word that is INCORRECTLY used is 25.____

A. *shall* in the 1st sentence
B. *voluntary* in the 3rd sentence
C. *occurred* in the 4th sentence
D. *intra-district* in the last sentence

KEY (CORRECT ANSWERS)

1. C
2. B
3. B
4. B
5. B
6. C
7. D
8. B
9. C
10. D
11. C
12. B
13. A
14. D
15. B
16. A
17. C
18. B
19. A
20. D
21. D
22. D
23. B
24. B
25. C

READING COMPREHENSION
UNDERSTANDING AND INTERPRETING WRITTEN MATERIAL
EXAMINATION SECTION
TEST 1

DIRECTIONS: Each question or incomplete statement is followed by several suggested answers or completions. Select the one that BEST answers the question or completes the statement. *PRINT THE LETTER OF THE CORRECT ANSWER IN THE SPACE AT THE RIGHT.*

Questions 1-2.

DIRECTIONS: Questions 1 and 2 are to be answered SOLELY on the basis of the following passage.

The employees in a unit or division of a government agency may be referred to as a work group. Within a government agency which has existed for some time, the work groups will have evolved traditions of their own. The persons in these work groups acquire these traditions as part of the process of work adjustment within their groups. Usually, a work group in a large organization will contain *oldtimers*, *newcomers*, and *in-betweeners*. Like the supervisor of a group, who is not necessarily an oldtimer or the oldest member, oldtimers usually have great influence. They can recall events unknown to others and are a storehouse of information and advice about current problems in the light of past experience. They pass along the traditions of the group to the others who, in turn, become oldtimers themselves. Thus, the traditions of the group which have been honored and revered by long acceptance are continued.

1. According to the above passage, the traditions of a work group within a government agency are developed 1._____

   A. at the time the group is established
   B. over a considerable period of time
   C. in order to give recognition to oldtimers
   D. for the group before it is established

2. According to the above passage, the oldtimers within a work group 2._____

   A. are the means by which long accepted practices and customs are perpetuated
   B. would best be able to settle current problems that arise
   C. are honored because of the changes they have made in the traditions
   D. have demonstrated that they have learned to do their work well

Questions 3-4.

DIRECTIONS: Questions 3 and 4 are to be answered SOLELY on the basis of the following passage.

In public agencies, the success of a person assigned to perform first-line supervisory duties depends in large part upon the personal relations between him and his subordinate employees. The goal of supervising effort is something more than to obtain compliance with procedures established by some central office. The major objective is work accomplishment. In order for this goal to be attained, employees must want to attain it and must exercise initiative in their work. Only if employees are generally satisfied with the type of supervision which exists in an organization will they put forth their best efforts.

3. According to the above passage, in order for employees to try to do their work as well as they can, it is essential that 3.____

   A. they participate in determining their working conditions and rates of pay
   B. their supervisors support the employees' viewpoints in meetings with higher management
   C. they are content with the supervisory practices which are being used
   D. their supervisors make the changes in working procedures that the employees request

4. It can be inferred from the above passage that the goals of a unit in a public agency will not be reached unless the employees in the unit 4.____

   A. wish to reach them and are given the opportunity to make individual contributions to the work
   B. understand the relationship between the goals of the unit and goals of the agency
   C. have satisfactory personal relationships with employees of other units in the agency
   D. carefully follow the directions issued by higher authorities

Questions 5-9.

DIRECTIONS: Questions 5 through 9 are to be answered SOLELY on the basis of the following passage.

If an employee thinks he can save money, time, or material for the city or has an idea about how to do something better than it is being done, he shouldn't keep it to himself. He should send his ideas to the Employees' Suggestion Program, using the special form which is kept on hand in all departments. An employee may send in as many ideas as he wishes. To make sure that each idea is judged fairly, the name of the suggester is not made known until an award is made. The awards are certificates of merit or cash prizes ranging from $10 to $500.

5. According to the above passage, an employee who knows how to do a job in a better way should 5.____

   A. be sure it saves enough time to be worthwhile
   B. get paid the money he saves for the city
   C. keep it to himself to avoid being accused of causing a speed-up
   D. send his idea to the Employees' Suggestion Program

6. In order to send his idea to the Employees' Suggestion Program, an employee should 6._____

   A. ask the Department of Personnel for a special form
   B. get the special form in his own department
   C. mail the idea using Special Delivery
   D. send it on plain, white letter-size paper

7. An employee may send to the Employees' Suggestion Program 7._____

   A. as many ideas as he can think of
   B. no more than one idea each week
   C. no more than ten ideas in a month
   D. only one idea on each part of the job

8. The reason the name of an employee who makes a suggestion is not made known at first is to 8._____

   A. give the employee a larger award
   B. help the judges give more awards
   C. insure fairness in judging
   D. only one idea on each part of the job

9. An employee whose suggestion receives an award may be given a 9._____

   A. bonus once a year
   B. certificate for $10
   C. cash prize of up to $500
   D. salary increase of $500

Questions 10-12.

DIRECTIONS: Questions 10 through 12 are to be answered SOLELY on the basis of the following passage.

According to the rules of the Department of Personnel, the work of every permanent city employee is reviewed and rated by his supervisor at least once a year. The civil service rating system gives the employee and his supervisor a chance to talk about the progress made during the past year as well as about those parts of the job in which the employee needs to do better. In order to receive a pay increase each year, the employee must have a satisfactory service rating. Service ratings also count toward an employee's final mark on a promotion examination.

10. According to the above passage, a permanent city employee is rated AT LEAST once 10._____

   A. before his work is reviewed
   B. every six months
   C. yearly by his supervisor
   D. yearly by the Department of Personnel

11. According to the above passage, under the rating system the supervisor and the employee can discuss how 11._____

   A. much more work needs to be done next year
   B. the employee did his work last year

C. the work can be made easier next year
D. the work of the Department can be increased

12. According to the above passage, a permanent city employee will NOT receive a yearly pay increase 12.____

A. if he received a pay increase the year before
B. if he used his service rating for his mark on a promotion examination
C. if his service rating is unsatisfactory
D. unless he got some kind of a service rating

Questions 13-16.

DIRECTIONS: Questions 13 through 16 are to be answered SOLELY on the basis of the following passage.

It is an accepted fact that the rank and file employee can frequently advance worthwhile suggestions toward increasing efficiency. For this reason, an Employees' Suggestion System has been developed and put into operation. Suitable means have been provided at each departmental location for the confidential submission of suggestions. Numerous suggestions have been received thus far and, after study, about five percent of the ideas submitted are being translated into action. It is planned to set up, eventually, monetary awards for all worthwhile suggestions.

13. According to the above passage, a MAJOR reason why an Employees' Suggestion System was established is that 13.____

A. an organized program of improvement is better than a haphazard one
B. employees can often give good suggestions to increase efficiency
C. once a fact is accepted, it is better to act on it than to do nothing
D. the suggestions of rank and file employees were being neglected

14. According to the above passage, under the Employees' Suggestion System, 14.____

A. a file of worthwhile suggestions will eventually be set up at each departmental location
B. it is possible for employees to turn in suggestions without fellow employees knowing of it
C. means have been provided for the regular and frequent collection of suggestions submitted
D. provision has been made for the judging of worthwhile suggestions by an Employees' Suggestion Committee

15. According to the above passage, it is reasonable to assume that 15.____

A. all suggestions must be turned in at a central office
B. employees who make worthwhile suggestions will be promoted
C. not all the prizes offered will be monetary ones
D. prizes of money will be given for the best suggestions

16. According to the above passage, of the many suggestions made, 16.____

    A. all are first tested
    B. a small part are put into use
    C. most are very worthwhile
    D. samples are studied

Questions 17-20.

DIRECTIONS: Questions 17 through 20 are to be answered SOLELY on the basis of the following passage.

Employees may be granted leaves of absence without pay at the discretion of the Personnel Officer. Such a leave without pay shall begin on the first working day on which the employee does not report for duty and shall continue to the first day on which the employee returns to duty. The Personnel Division may vary the dates of the leave for the record so as to conform with payroll periods, but in no case shall an employee be off the payroll for a different number of calendar days than would have been the case if the actual dates mentioned above had been used. An employee who has vacation or overtime to his credit, which is available for normal use, may take time off immediately prior to beginning a leave of absence without pay, chargeable against all or part of such vacation or overtime.

17. According to the above passage, the Personnel Officer must 17.____

    A. decide if a leave of absence without pay should be granted
    B. require that a leave end on the last working day of a payroll period
    C. see to it that a leave of absence begins on the first working day of a pay period
    D. vary the dates of a leave of absence to conform with a payroll period

18. According to the above passage, the exact dates of a leave of absence without pay may be varied provided that the 18.____

    A. calendar days an employee is off the payroll equal the actual leave granted
    B. leave conforms to an even number of payroll periods
    C. leave when granted made provision for variance to simplify payroll records
    D. Personnel Officer approves the variation

19. According to the above passage, a leave of absence without pay must extend from the 19.____

    A. first day of a calendar period to the first day the employee resumes work
    B. first day of a payroll period to the last calendar day of the leave
    C. first working day missed to the first day on which the employee resumes work
    D. last day on which an employee works through the first day he returns to work

20. According to the above passage, an employee may take extra time off just before the start of a leave of absence without pay if 20.____

    A. he charges this extra time against his leave
    B. he has a favorable balance of vacation or overtime which has been frozen
    C. the vacation or overtime that he would normally use for a leave without pay has not been charged in this way before
    D. there is time to his credit which he may use

Question 21.

DIRECTIONS: Question 21 is to be answered SOLELY on the basis of the following passage.

In considering those things which are motivators and incentives to work, it might be just as erroneous not to give sufficient weight to money as an incentive as it is to give too much weight. It is not a problem of establishing a rank-order of importance, but one of knowing that motivation is a blend or mixture rather than a pure element. It is simple to say that cultural factors count more than financial considerations, but this leads only to the conclusion that our society is financial-oriented.

21. Based on the above passage, in our society, cultural and social motivations to work are 21.____

A. things which cannot be avoided
B. melded to financial incentives
C. of less consideration than high pay
D. not balanced equally with economic or financial considerations

Question 22.

DIRECTIONS: Question 22 is to be answered SOLELY on the basis of the following passage.

A general principle of training and learning with respect to people is that they learn more readily if they receive *feedback.* Essential to maintaining proper motivational levels is knowledge of results which indicate level of progress. Feedback also assists the learning process by identifying mistakes. If this kind of information were not given to the learner, then improper or inappropriate job performance may be instilled.

22. Based on the above passage, which of the following is MOST accurate? 22.____

A. Learning will not take place without feedback.
B. In the absence of feedback, improper or inappropriate job performance will be learned.
C. To properly motivate a learner, the learner must have his progress made known to him.
D. Trainees should be told exactly what to do if they are to learn properly.

Question 23.

DIRECTIONS: Question 23 is to be answered SOLELY on the basis of the following passage.

In a democracy, the obligation of public officials is twofold. They must not only do an efficient and satisfactory job of administration, but also they must persuade the public that it is an efficient and satisfactory job. It is a burden which, if properly assumed, will make democracy work and perpetuate reform government.

23. The above passage means that 23.____

A. public officials should try to please everybody
B. public opinion is instrumental in determining the policy of public officials

C. satisfactory performance of the job of administration will eliminate opposition to its work
D. frank and open procedure in a public agency will aid in maintaining progressive government

Question 24.

DIRECTIONS: Question 24 is to be answered SOLELY on the basis of the following passage.

Upon retirement for service, a member shall receive a retirement allowance which shall consist of an annuity which shall be the actuarial equivalent of his accumulated deductions at the time of his retirement and a pension, in addition to his annuity, which shall be equal to one service-fraction of his final compensation, multiplied by the number of years of service since he last became a member credited to him, and a pension which is the actuarial equivalent of the reserve-for-increased-take-home-pay to which he may then be entitled, if any.

24. According to the above passage, a retirement allowance shall consist of a(n) 24.____

A. annuity, plus a pension, plus an actuarial equivalent
B. annuity, plus a pension, plus reserve-for-increased-take-home-pay, if any
C. annuity, plus reserve-for-increased-take-home-pay, if any, plus final compensation
D. pension, plus reserve-for-increased-take-home-pay, if any, plus accumulated deductions

Question 25.

DIRECTIONS: Question 25 is to be answered SOLELY on the basis of the following passage.

Membership in the retirement system shall cease upon the occurrence of any one of the following conditions: when the time out of service of any member who has total service of less than 25 years, shall aggregate more than 5 years; when the time out of service of any member who has total service of 25 years or more, shall aggregate more than 10 years; when any member shall have withdrawn more than 50% of his accumulated deductions; or when any member shall have withdrawn the cash benefit provided by Section B3-35.0 of the Administrative Code.

25. According to the information in the above passage, membership in the retirement system shall cease when an employee 25.____

A. with 17 years of service has been on a leave of absence for 3 years
B. withdraws 50% of his accumulated deductions
C. with 28 years of service has been out of service for 10 years
D. withdraws his cash benefits

KEY (CORRECT ANSWERS)

1. B
2. A
3. C
4. A
5. D
6. B
7. A
8. C
9. B
10. C
11. B
12. C
13. B
14. B
15. D
16. B
17. A
18. A
19. C
20. D
21. B
22. C
23. D
24. B
25. D

TEST 2

DIRECTIONS: Each question or incomplete statement is followed by several suggested answers or completions. Select the one that BEST answers the question or completes the statement. *PRINT THE LETTER OF THE CORRECT ANSWER IN THE SPACE AT THE RIGHT.*

Questions 1-6.

DIRECTIONS: Questions 1 through 6 are to be answered SOLELY on the basis of the following passage from an old office manual.

Since almost every office has some contact with data-processed records, a stenographer should have some understanding of the basic operations of data processing. Data processing systems now handle about one-third of all office paperwork. On punched cards, magnetic tape, or on other mediums, data are recorded before being fed into the computer for processing. A machine such as the keypunch is used to convert the data written on the source document into the coded symbols on punched cards or tapes. After data has been converted, it must be verified to guarantee absolute accuracy of conversion. In this manner, data becomes a permanent record which can be read by electronic computers that compare, store, compute, and otherwise process data at high speeds.

One key person in a computer installation is a programmer, the man or woman who puts business and scientific problems into special symbolic languages that can be read by the computer. Jobs done by the computer range all the way from payroll operations to chemical process control, but most computer applications are directed toward management data. About half of the programmers employed by business come to their positions with college degrees; the remaining half are promoted to their positions from within the organization on the basis of demonstrated ability without regard to education.

1. Of the following, the BEST title for the above passage is 1.____

   A. THE STENOGRAPHER AS DATA PROCESSOR
   B. THE RELATION OF KEYPUNCHING TO STENOGRAPHY
   C. UNDERSTANDING DATA PROCESSING
   D. PERMANENT OFFICE RECORDS

2. According to the above passage, a stenographer should understand the basic operations of data processing because 2.____

   A. almost every office today has contact with data processed by computer
   B. any office worker may be asked to verify the accuracy of data
   C. most offices are involved in the production of permanent records
   D. data may be converted into computer language by typing on a keypunch

3. According to the above passage, the data which the computer understands is MOST often expressed as 3.____

   A. a scientific programming language
   B. records or symbols punched on tape, cards, or other mediums
   C. records on cards
   D. records on tape

4. According to the above passage, computers are used MOST often to handle 4.____

   A. management data
   B. problems of higher education
   C. the control of chemical processes
   D. payroll operations

5. Computer programming is taught in many colleges and business schools. 5.____
   The above passage implies that programmers in industry

   A. must have professional training
   B. need professional training to advance
   C. must have at least a college education to do adequate programming tasks
   D. do not need college education to do programming work

6. According to the above passage, data to be processed by computer should be 6.____

   A. recent
   B. basic
   C. complete
   D. verified

Questions 7-10.

DIRECTIONS: Questions 7 through 10 are to be answered SOLELY on the basis of the following passage.

There is nothing that will take the place of good sense on the part of the stenographer. You may be perfect in transcribing exactly what the dictator says and your speed may be adequate, but without an understanding of the dictator's intent as well as his words, you are likely to be a mediocre secretary.

A serious error that is made when taking dictation is putting down something that does not make sense. Most people who dictate material would rather be asked to repeat and explain than to receive transcribed material which has errors due to inattention or doubt. Many dictators request that their grammar be corrected by their secretaries, but unless specifically asked to do so, secretaries should not do it without first checking with the dictator. Secretaries should be aware that, in some cases, dictators may use incorrect grammar or slang expressions to create a particular effect.

Some people dictate commas, periods, and paragraphs, while others expect the stenographer to know when, where, and how to punctuate. A well-trained secretary should be able to indicate the proper punctuation by listening to the pauses and tones of the dictator's voice.

A stenographer who has taken dictation from the same person for a period of time should be able to understand him under most conditions, By increasing her tact, alertness, and efficiency, a secretary can become more competent.

7. According to the above passage, which of the following statements concerning the dictation of punctuation is CORRECT? 7.____

   A. Dictator may use incorrect punctuation to create a desired style
   B. Dictator should indicate all punctuation
   C. Stenographer should know how to punctuate based on the pauses and tones of the dictator
   D. Stenographer should not type any punctuation if it has not been dictated to her

8. According to the above passage, how should secretaries handle grammatical errors in a dictation? Secretaries should 8.____

   A. *not correct* grammatical errors unless the dictator is aware that this is being done
   B. *correct* grammatical errors by having the dictator repeat the line with proper pauses
   C. *correct* grammatical errors if they have checked the correctness in a grammar book
   D. *correct* grammatical errors based on their own good sense

9. If a stenographer is confused about the method of spacing and indenting of a report which has just been dictated to her, she GENERALLY should 9.____

   A. do the best she can
   B. ask the dictator to explain what she should do
   C. try to improve her ability to understand dictated material
   D. accept the fact that her stenographic ability is not adequate

10. In the last line of the first paragraph, the word *mediocre* means MOST NEARLY 10.____

   A. superior
   B. respected
   C. disregarded
   D. second-rate

Questions 11-12.

DIRECTIONS: Questions 11 and 12 are to be answered SOLELY on the basis of the following passage.

The number of legible carbon copies required to be produced determines the weight of the carbon paper to be used. When only one copy is made, heavy carbon paper is satisfactory. Most typists, however, use medium-weight carbon paper and find it serviceable for up to three or four copies. If five or more copies are to be made, it is wise to use light carbon paper. On the other hand, the finish of carbon paper to be used depends largely on the stroke of the typist and, in lesser degree, on the number of copies to be made and on whether the typewriter has pica or elite type. A soft-finish carbon paper should be used if the typist's touch is light or if a noiseless machine is used. It is desirable for the average typist to use medium-finish carbon paper for ordinary work, when only a few carbon copies are required. Elite type requires a harder carbon finish than pica type for the same number of copies.

11. According to the above passage, the lighter the carbon paper used, 11.____

   A. the softer the finish of the carbon paper will be
   B. the greater the number of legible carbon copies that can be made
   C. the greater the number of times the carbon paper can be used
   D. the lighter the typist's touch should be

12. According to the above passage, the MOST important factor which determines whether the finish of carbon paper to be used in typing should be hard, medium, or soft is 12.____

   A. the touch of the typist
   B. the number of carbon copies required
   C. whether the type in the typewriter is pica or elite
   D. whether a machine with pica type will produce the same number of carbon copies as a machine with elite type

Questions 13-16.

DIRECTIONS: Questions 13 through 16 are to be answered SOLELY on the basis of the following passage.

Modern office methods, geared to ever higher speeds and aimed at ever greater efficiency, are largely the result of the typewriter. The typewriter is a substitute for handwriting and, in the hands of a skilled typist, not only turns out letters and other documents at least three times faster than a penman can do the work, but turns out the greater volume more uniformly and legibly. With the use of carbon paper and onionskin paper, identical copies can be made at the same time.

The typewriter, besides its effect on the conduct of business and government, has had a very important effect on the position of women. The typewriter has done much to bring women into business and government, and today there are vastly more women than men typists. Many women have used the keys of the typewriter to climb the ladder to responsible managerial positions.

The typewriter, as its name implies, employs type to make an ink impression on paper. For many years, the manual typewriter was the standard machine used. Today, the electric typewriter is dominant, and completely automatic electronic typewriters are coming into wider use.

The mechanism of the office manual typewriter includes a set of keys arranged systematically in rows; a semicircular frame of type, connected to the keys by levers; the carriage, or paper carrier; a rubber roller, called a platen, against which the type strikes; and an inked ribbon which make the impression of the type character when the key strikes it.

13. The above passage mentions a number of good features of the combination of a skilled typist and a typewriter. Of the following, the feature which is NOT mentioned in the passage is 13.____

A. speed B. reliability
C. uniformity D. legibility

14. According to the above passage, a skilled typist can 14.____

A. turn out at least five carbon copies of typed matter
B. type at least three times faster than a penman can write
C. type more than 80 words a minute
D. readily move into a managerial position

15. According to the above passage, which of the following is NOT part of the mechanism of a manual typewriter? 15.____

A. Carbon paper B. Platen
C. Paper carrier D. Inked ribbon

16. According to the above passage, the typewriter has helped 16.____

A. men more than women in business
B. women in career advancement into management
C. men and women equally, but women have taken better advantage of it
D. more women than men, because men generally dislike routine typing work

Questions 17-21.

DIRECTIONS: Questions 17 through 21 are to be answered SOLELY on the basis of the following passage.

The recipient gains an impression of a typewritten letter before he begins to read the message. Factors which provide for a good first impression include margins and spacing that are visually pleasing, formal parts of the letter which are correctly placed according to the style of the letter, copy which is free of obvious erasures and over-strikes, and transcript that is even and clear. The problem for the typist is that of how to produce that first, positive impression of her work.

There are several general rules which a typist can follow when she wishes to prepare a properly spaced letter on a sheet of letterhead. Ordinarily, the width of a letter should not be less than four inches nor more than six inches. The side margins should also have a desirable relation to the bottom margin and the space between the letterhead and the body of the letter. Usually the most appealing arrangement is when the side margins are even and the bottom margin is slightly wider than the side margins. In some offices, however, standard line length is used for all business letters, and the secretary then varies the spacing between the date line and the inside address according to the length of the letter.

17. The BEST title for the above passage would be 17.____

A. WRITING OFFICE LETTERS
B. MAKING GOOD FIRST IMPRESSIONS
C. JUDGING WELL-TYPED LETTERS
D. GOOD PLACING AND SPACING FOR OFFICE LETTERS

18. According to the above passage, which of the following might be considered the way in which people very quickly judge the quality of work which has been typed? By 18.____

A. measuring the margins to see if they are correct
B. looking at the spacing and cleanliness of the typescript
C. scanning the body of the letter for meaning
D. reading the date line and address for errors

19. What, according to the above passage, would be definitely UNDESIRABLE as the average line length of a typed letter? 19.____

A. 4"
B. 6"
C. 5"
D. 7"

20. According to the above passage, when the line length is kept standard, the secretary 20.____

A. does not have to vary the spacing at all since this also is standard
B. adjusts the spacing between the date line and inside address for different lengths of letters
C. uses the longest line as a guideline for spacing between the date line and inside address
D. varies-the number of spaces between the lines

21. According to the above passage, side margins are MOST pleasing when they 21.____

A. are even and somewhat smaller than the bottom margin
B. are slightly wider than the bottom margin
C. vary with the length of the letter
D. are figured independently from the letterhead and the body of the letter

Questions 22-25.

DIRECTIONS: Questions 22 through 25 are to be answered SOLELY on the basis of the following passage.

Typed pages can reflect the simplicity of modern art in a machine age. Lightness and evenness can be achieved by proper layout and balance of typed lines and white space. Instead of solid, cramped masses of uneven, crowded typing, there should be a pleasing balance up and down as well as horizontal.

To have real balance, your page must have a center. The eyes see the center of the sheet slightly above the real center. This is the way both you and the reader see it. Try imagining a line down the center of the page that divides the paper in equal halves. On either side of your paper, white space and blocks of typing need to be similar in size and shape. Although left and right margins should be equal, top and bottom margins need not be as exact. It looks better to hold a bottom border wider than a top margin, so that your typing rests upon a cushion of white space. To add interest to the appearance of the page, try making one paragraph between one-half and two-thirds the size of an adjacent paragraph.

Thus, by taking full advantage of your typewriter, the pages that you type will not only be accurate but will also be attractive.

22. It can be inferred from the above passage that the basic importance of proper balancing on a typed page is that proper balancing 22.____

A. makes a typed page a work of modern art
B. provides exercise in proper positioning of a typewriter
C. increases the amount of typed copy on the paper
D. draws greater attention and interest to the page

23. A reader will tend to see the center of a typed page 23.____

A. somewhat higher than the true center
B. somewhat lower than the true center
C. on either side of the true center
D. about two-thirds of an inch above the true center

24. Which of the following suggestions is NOT given by the above passage? 24.____

A. Bottom margins may be wider than top borders.
B. Keep all paragraphs approximately the same size.
C. Divide your page with an imaginary line down the middle.
D. Side margins should be equalized.

25. Of the following, the BEST title for the above passage is 25.____

A. INCREASING THE ACCURACY OF THE TYPED PAGE
B. DETERMINATION OF MARGINS FOR TYPED COPY
C. LAYOUT AND BALANCE OF THE TYPED PAGE
D. HOW TO TAKE FULL ADVANTAGE OF THE TYPEWRITER

KEY (CORRECT ANSWERS)

1.	C	11.	B
2.	A	12.	A
3.	B	13.	C
4.	A	14.	B
5.	D	15.	A
6.	D	16.	B
7.	C	17.	D
8.	A	18.	B
9.	B	19.	D
10.	D	20.	B

21. A
22. D
23. A
24. B
25. C

TEST 3

DIRECTIONS: Each question or incomplete statement is followed by several suggested answers or completions. Select the one that BEST answers the question or completes the statement. *PRINT THE LETTER OF THE CORRECT ANSWER IN THE SPACE AT THE RIGHT.*

Questions 1-5.

DIRECTIONS: Questions 1 through 5 are to be answered SOLELY on the basis of the following passage.

A written report is a communication of information from one person to another. It is an account of some matter especially investigated, however routine that matter may be. The ultimate basis of any good written report is facts, which become known through observation and verification. Good written reports may seem to be no more than general ideas and opinions. However, in such cases, the facts leading to these opinions were gathered, verified, and reported earlier, and the opinions are dependent upon these facts. Good style, proper form, and emphasis cannot make a good written report out of unreliable information and bad judgment; but on the other hand, solid investigation and brilliant thinking are not likely to become very useful until they are effectively communicated to others. If a person's work calls for written reports, then his work is often no better than his written reports.

1. Based on the information in the above passage, it can be concluded that opinions expressed in a report should be 1.____

   A. based on facts which are gathered and reported
   B. emphasized repeatedly when they result from a special investigation
   C. kept to a minimum
   D. separated from the body of the report

2. In the above passage, the one of the following which is mentioned as a way of establishing facts is 2.____

   A. authority B. reporting
   C. communication D. verification

3. According to the above passage, the characteristic shared by ALL written reports is that they are 3.____

   A. accounts of routine matters B. transmissions of information
   C. reliable and logical D. written in proper form

4. Which of the following conclusions can logically be drawn from the information given in the above passage? 4.____

   A. Brilliant thinking can make up for unreliable information in a report.
   B. One method of judging an individual's work is the quality of the written reports he is required to submit.
   C. Proper form and emphasis can make a good report out of unreliable information.
   D. Good written reports that seem to be no more than general ideas should be rewritten.

5. Which of the following suggested titles would be MOST appropriate for the above passage? 5.___

   A. GATHERING AND ORGANIZING FACTS
   B. TECHNIQUES OF OBSERVATION
   C. NATURE AND PURPOSE OF REPORTS
   D. REPORTS AND OPINIONS: DIFFERENCES AND SIMILARITIES

Questions 6-8.

DIRECTIONS: Questions 6 through 8 are to be answered SOLELY on the basis of the following passage.

The most important unit of the mimeograph machine is a perforated metal drum over which is stretched a cloth ink pad. A reservoir inside the drum contains the ink which flows through the perforations and saturates the ink pad. To operate the machine, the operator first removes from the machine the protective sheet, which keeps the ink from drying while the machine is not in use. He then hooks the stencil face down on the drum, draws the stencil smoothly over the drum, and fastens the stencil at the bottom. The speed with which the drum turns determines the blackness of the copies printed. Slow turning gives heavy, black copies; fast turning gives light, clear-cut reproductions. If reproductions are run on other than porous paper, slip-sheeting is necessary to prevent smearing. Often, the printed copy fails to drop readily as it comes from the machine. This may be due to static electricity. To remedy this difficulty, the operator fastens a strip of tinsel from side to side near the impression roller so that the printed copy just touches the soft stems of the tinsel as it is ejected from the machine, thus grounding the static electricity to the frame of the machine.

6. According to the above passage, 6.___

   A. turning the drum fast produces light copies
   B. stencils should be placed face up on the drum
   C. ink pads should be changed daily
   D. slip-sheeting is necessary when porous paper is being used

7. According to the above passage, when a mimeograph machine is not in use, 7.___

   A. the ink should be drained from the drum
   B. the ink pad should be removed
   C. the machine should be covered with a protective sheet
   D. the counter should be set at zero

8. According to the above passage, static electricity is grounded to the frame of the mimeograph machine by means of 8.___

   A. a slip-sheeting device
   B. a strip of tinsel
   C. an impression roller
   D. hooks located at the top of the drum

Questions 9-10.

DIRECTIONS: Questions 9 and 10 are to be answered SOLELY on the basis of the following passage.

The proofreading of material typed from copy is performed more accurately and more speedily when two persons perform this work as a team. The person who did not do the typing should read aloud the original copy while the person who did the typing should check the reading against the typed copy. The reader should speak very slowly and repeat the figures, using a different grouping of numbers when repeating the figures. For example, in reading 1967, the reader may say *one-nine-six-seven* on first reading the figure and *nineteen-sixty-seven* on repeating the figure. The reader should read all punctuation marks, taking nothing for granted. Since mistakes can occur anywhere, everything typed should be proofread. To avoid confusion, the proofreading team should use the standard proofreading marks, which are given in most dictionaries.

9. According to the above passage, the 9.____

   A. person who holds the typed copy is called the reader
   B. two members of a proofreading team should take turns in reading the typed copy aloud
   C. typed copy should be checked by the person who did the typing
   D. person who did not do the typing should read aloud from the typed copy

10. According to the above passage, 10.____

    A. it is unnecessary to read the period at the end of a sentence
    B. typographical errors should be noted on the original copy
    C. each person should develop his own set of proofreading marks
    D. figures should be read twice

Questions 11-16.

DIRECTIONS: Questions 11 through 16 are to be answered SOLELY on the basis of the above passage.

Basic to every office is the need for proper lighting. Inadequate lighting is a familiar cause of fatigue and serves to create a somewhat dismal atmosphere in the office. One requirement of proper lighting is that it be of an appropriate intensity. Intensity is measured in foot candles. According to the Illuminating Engineering Society of New York, for casual seeing tasks such as in reception rooms, inactive file rooms, and other service areas, it is recommended that the amount of light be 30 foot-candles. For ordinary seeing tasks such as reading, work in active file rooms, and in mailrooms, the recommended lighting is 100 foot-candles. For very difficult seeing tasks such as accounting, transcribing, and business machine use, the recommended lighting is 150 foot-candles.

Lighting intensity is only one requirement. Shadows and glare are to be avoided. For example, the larger the proportion of a ceiling filled with lighting units, the more glare-free and comfortable the lighting will be. Natural lighting from windows is not too dependable because on dark wintry days, windows yield little usable light, and on sunny summer afternoons, the glare from windows may be very distracting. Desks should not face the windows. Finally, the main lighting source ought to be overhead and to the left of the user,

11. According to the above passage, insufficient light in the office may cause 11.____

A. glare
B. tiredness
C. shadows
D. distraction

12. Based on the above passage, which of the following must be considered when planning lighting arrangements? The 12.____

A. amount of natural light present
B. amount of work to be done
C. level of difficulty of work to be done
D. type of activity to be carried out

13. It can be inferred from the above passage that a well-coordinated lighting scheme is LIKELY to result in 13.____

A. greater employee productivity
B. elimination of light reflection
C. lower lighting cost
D. more use of natural light

14. Of the following, the BEST title for the above passage is 14.____

A. CHARACTERISTICS OF LIGHT
B. LIGHT MEASUREMENT DEVICES
C. FACTORS TO CONSIDER WHEN PLANNING LIGHTING SYSTEMS
D. COMFORT VS. COST WHEN DEVISING LIGHTING ARRANGEMENTS

15. According to the above passage, a foot-candle is a measurement of the 15.____

A. number of bulbs used
B. strength of the light
C. contrast between glare and shadow
D. proportion of the ceiling filled with lighting units

16. According to the above passage, the number of foot-candles of light that would be needed to copy figures onto a payroll is ______ foot-candles. 16.____

A. less than 30
B. 100
C. 30
D. 150

Questions 17-23.

DIRECTIONS: Questions 17 through 23 are to be answered SOLELY on the basis of the following passage, which is the Fee Schedule of a hypothetical college.

FEE SCHEDULE

A. A candidate for any baccalaureate degree is not required to pay tuition fees for undergraduate courses until he exceeds 128 credits, Candidates exceeding 128 credits in undergraduate courses are charged at the rate of $100 a credit for each credit of undergraduate course work in excess of 128. Candidates for a baccalaureate degree who are taking graduate courses must pay the same fee as any other student taking graduate courses
B. Non-degree students and college graduates are charged tuition fees for courses, whether undergraduate or graduate, at the rate of $180 a credit. For such students, there is an additional charge of $150 for each class hour per week in excess of the number of course credits. For example, if a three-credit course meets five hours a week, there is an additional charge for the extra two hours. Graduate courses are shown with a (G) before the course number.
C. All students are required to pay the laboratory fees indicated after the number of credits given for that course.
D. All students must pay a $250 general fee each semester.
E. Candidates for a baccalaureate degree are charged a $150 medical insurance fee for each semester. All other students are charged a $100 medical insurance fee each semester.

17. Miss Burton is not a candidate for a degree. She registers for the following courses in the spring semester: Economics 12, 4 hours a week, 3 credits; History (G) 23, 4 hours a week, 3 credits; English 1, 2 hours a week, 2 credits. The TOTAL amount in fees that Miss Burton must pay is 17.____

A. less than $2000
B. at least $2000 but less than $2100
C. at least $2100 but less than $2200
D. $2200 or over

18. Miss Gray is not a candidate for a degree. She registers for the following courses in the fall semester: History 3, 3 hours a week, 3 credits; English 5, 3 hours a week, 2 credits; Physics 5, 6 hours a week, 3 credits, laboratory fee $ 60; Mathematics 7, 4 hours a week, 3 credits. The TOTAL amount in fees that Miss Gray must pay is 18.____

A. less than $3150
B. at least $3150 but less than $3250
C. at least $3250 but less than $3350
D. $3350 or over

19. Mr. Wall is a candidate for the Bachelor of Arts degree and has completed 126 credits. He registers for the following courses in the spring semester, his final semester at college: French 4, 3 hours a week, 3 credits; Physics (G) 15, 6 hours a week, 3 credits, laboratory fee $80; History (G) 33, 4 hours a week, 3 credits. The TOTAL amount in fees that this candidate must pay is 19.____

A. less than $2100
B. at least $2100 but less than $2300
C. at least $2300 but less than $2500
D. $2500

20. Mr. Tindall, a candidate for the B.A. degree, has completed 122 credits of undergraduate courses. He registers for the following courses in his final semester: English 31, 3 hours a week, 3 credits; Philosophy 12, 4 hours a week, 4 credits; Anthropology 15, 3 hours a week, 3 credits; Economics (G) 68, 3 hours a week, 3 credits. The TOTAL amount in fees that Mr. Tindall must pay in his final semester is 20.____

A. less than $1200
B. at least $1200 but less than $1400
C. at least $1400 but less than $1600
D. $1600

21. Mr. Cantrell, who was graduated from the college a year ago, registers for graduate courses in the fall semester. Each course for which he registers carries the same number of credits as the number of hours a week it meets. 21.____
If he pays a total of $1530; including a $100 laboratory fee, the number of credits for which he is registered is

A. 4 B. 5 C. 6 D. 7

22. Miss Jayson, who is not a candidate for a degree, has, registered for several courses including a lecture course in History. She withdraws from the course in History for which she had paid the required course fee of $690. The number of hours that this course is scheduled to meet is 22.____

A. 4 B. 5 C. 2 D. 3

23. Mr. Van Arsdale, a graduate of a college is Iowa, registers for the following courses in one semester: Chemistry 35, 5 hours a week, 3 credits; Biology 13, 4 hours a week, 3 credits, laboratory fee $150; Mathematics (G) 179, 3 hours a week, 3 credits. 23.____
The TOTAL amount in fees that Mr. Van Arsdale must pay is

A. less than $2400
B. at least $2400 but less than $2500
C. at least $2500 but less than $2600
D. at least $2600 or over

Questions 24-25.

DIRECTIONS: Questions 24 and 25 are to be answered SOLELY on the basis of the following passage.

A duplex envelope is an envelope composed of two sections securely fastened together so that they become one mailing piece. This type of envelope makes it possible for a first class letter to be delivered simultaneously with third or fourth class matter and yet not require payment of the much higher first class postage rate on the entire mailing. First class postage is paid only on the letter which goes in the small compartment, third or fourth class postage being paid on the contents of the larger compartment. The larger compartment generally has an ungummed flap or clasp for sealing. The first class or smaller compartment has a gummed flap for sealing. Postal regulations require that the exact amount of postage applicable to each compartment be separately attached to it.

24. On the basis of the above passage, it is MOST accurate to state that 24.____

A. the smaller compartment is placed inside the larger compartment before mailing
B. the two compartments may be detached and mailed separately
C. two classes of mailing matter may be mailed as a unit at two different postage rates
D. the more expensive postage rate is paid on the matter in the larger compartment

25. When a duplex envelope is used, the 25.____

A. first class compartment may be sealed with a clasp
B. correct amount of postage must be placed on each compartment
C. compartment containing third or fourth class mail requires a gummed flap for sealing
D. full amount of postage for both compartments may be placed on the larger compartment

---

KEY (CORRECT ANSWERS)

1.	A	11.	C
2.	D	12.	D
3.	B	13.	A
4.	B	14.	C
5.	C	15.	B
6.	A	16.	D
7.	C	17.	B
8.	B	18.	A
9.	C	19.	B
10.	D	20.	B

21. C
22. A
23. C
24. C
25. B

INTERPRETING STATISTICAL DATA
GRAPHS, CHARTS AND TABLES
TEST 1

DIRECTIONS: Each question or incomplete statement is followed by several suggested answers or completions. Select the one that BEST answers the question or completes the statement. *PRINT THE LETTER OF THE CORRECT ANSWER IN THE SPACE AT THE RIGHT.*

1. The following chart shows the number of persons employed in a certain industry for each year from 2007 through 2012. 1.____

	Thousands of Employees
2007	5.7
2008	6.8
2009	7.0
2010	7.1
2011	7.4
2012	6.4

In making a forecast of future trends, the one of the following steps which should be taken FIRST is to

A. take the six-year average
B. fit a curvilinear trend to the data
C. fit a straight line, omitting 2012 as an *outlier,* i.e., as an unusually low reading
D. check on what happened to the industry in 2012

2. Of the following concepts, the one which CANNOT be represented suitably by a pie chart is 2.____

A. percent shares
B. shares in absolute units
C. time trends
D. successive totals over time, with their shares

3. A pictogram is ESSENTIALLY another version of a(n)______ chart. 3.____

A. plain bar
B. component bar
C. pie
D. area

4. A time series for a certain cost is presented in a graph. It is drawn so that the vertical (cost) axis starts at a point well above zero. 4.____
This is a legitimate method of presentation for some purposes, but it may have the effect of

A. hiding fixed components of the cost
B. exaggerating changes which, in actual amounts, may be insignificant
C. magnifying fixed components of the cost
D. impairing correlation analysis

5. Certain budgetary data may be represented by bar, area or volume charts. Which one of the following BEST expresses the most appropriate order of usefulness? 5.____

A. Descends from bar to volume and area charts, the last two being about the same
B. Descends from volume to area to bar charts
C. Depends on the nature of the data presented
D. Descends from bar to area to volume charts

Questions 6-7.

DIRECTIONS: Questions 6 and 7 are to be answered on the basis of the layout below.

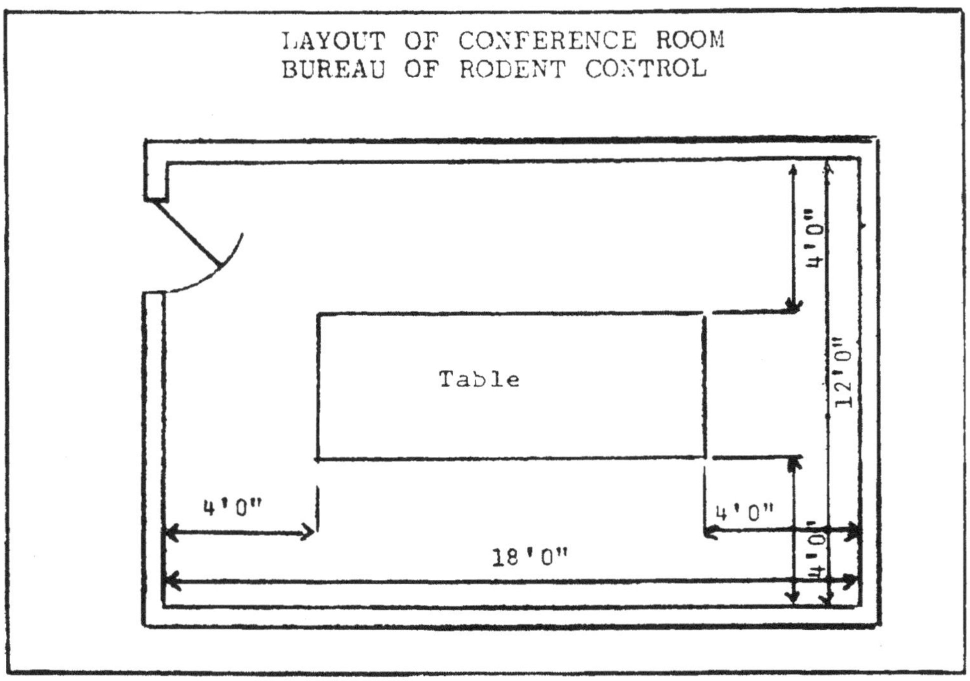

6. The LARGEST number of persons that can be accommodated in the area shown in the layout is 6.____

A. 16 B. 10 C. 8 D. 6

7. Assume that the Bureau's programs undergo expansion and the Director indicates that the feasibility of increasing the size of the conference room should be explored. For every two additional persons that are to be accommodated, the analyst should recommend that ______ be added to table length and ______ be added to room length. 7.____

A. 2'-6"; 2'-6"
B. 5'-0"; 5'-0"
C. 2'-6"; 5'-0"
D. 5'-0"; 2'-6"

Questions 8-9.

DIRECTIONS: Questions 8 and 9 are to be answered on the basis of the following groups, both of which depict the same information in different ways. The x and y axes in graphs A and B are not necessarily drawn in the same scale. The points along the curves on both graphs represent corresponding points and are the upper limits of class intervals.

GRAPH A

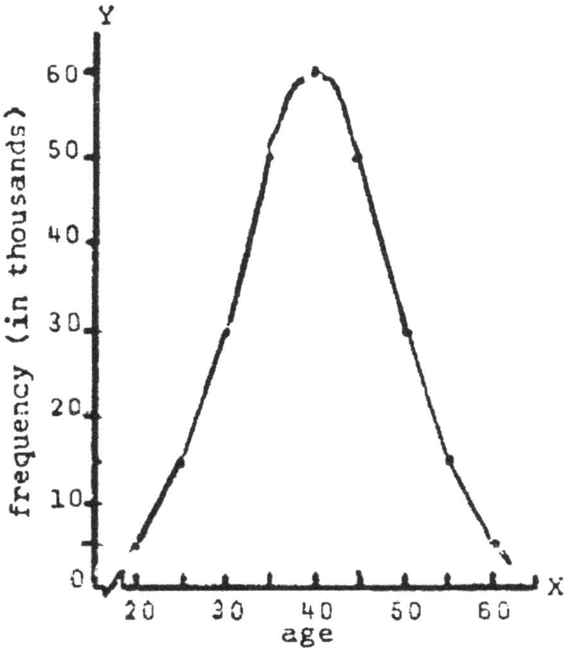

GRAPH B

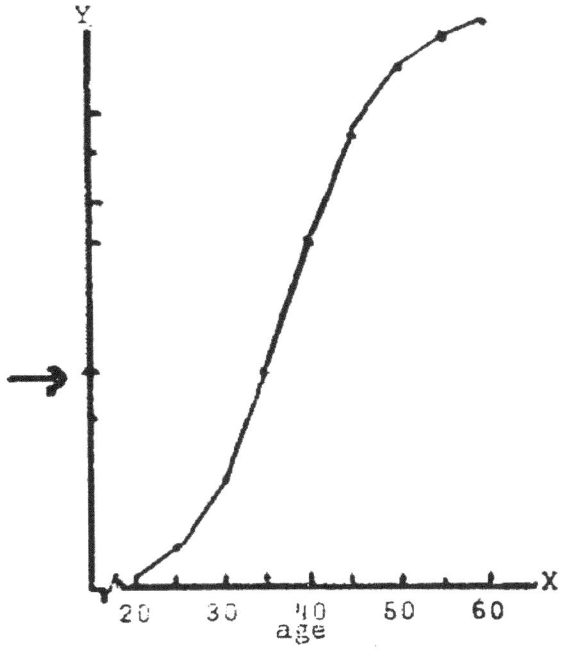

8. The ordinate (y-axis) in graph B is 8._____

A. frequency B. cumulative frequency
C. average frequency D. log frequency

9. The arrow on the y-axis in graph B indicates a particular number. That number is MOST NEARLY 9._____

A. 100 B. 50,000 C. 100,000 D. 150,000

Questions 10-11.

DIRECTIONS: Questions 10 and 11 are to be answered on the basis of the graphs below.

ROAD REPAIR COSTS IF PERFORMED BY
CITY STAFF OR AN OUTSIDE CONTRACTOR

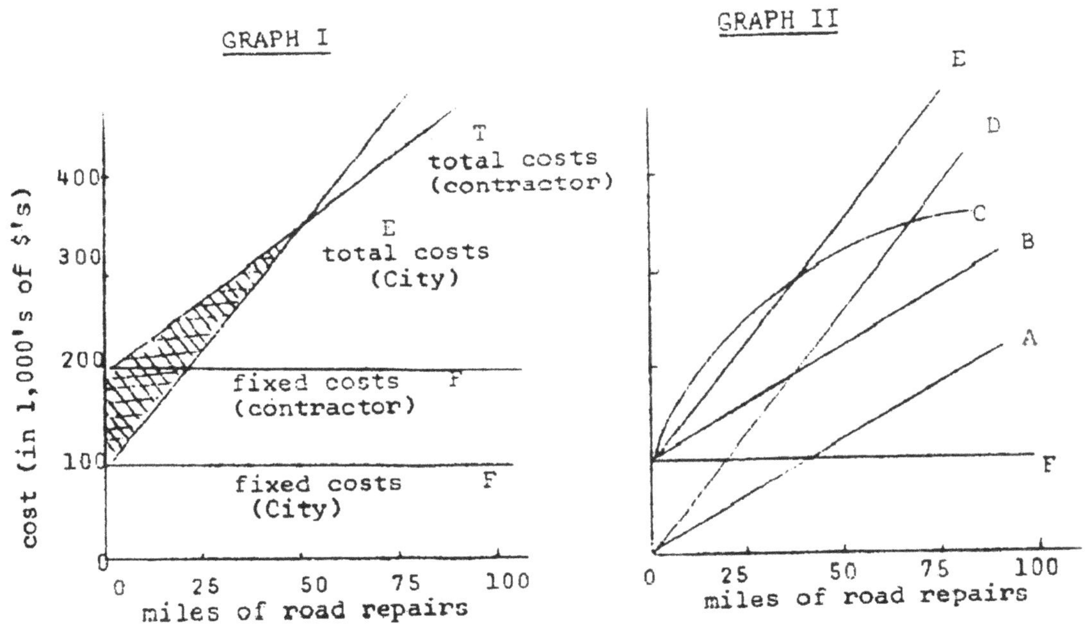

10. In Graph I, the vertical distance between lines E and T within the crosshatched area represents the _______ than 50 miles is performed by the city. 10.____

A. savings to the city if work of less
B. loss to the city if work of less
C. savings to the city if work of more
D. loss to the city if work of more

11. Graph II is identical to Graph I except that contractor costs have been eliminated. Total costs (line E) are the sum of fixed costs (line F) a.nd variable costs. Variable costs are represented by line 11.____

A. A B. B C. C D. D

Questions 12-13.

DIRECTIONS: Questions 12 and 13 are to be answered on the basis of the following chart. In a hypothetical problem involving four criteria and four alternatives, the following data have been assembled.

Cost Criterion	Effectiveness Criterion	Timing Criterion	Feasibility Criterion
Alternative A $500,000	50 units	3 months	probably feasible
Alternative B $300,000	100 units	6 months	probably feasible
Alternative C $400,000	50 units	12 months	probably infeasible
Alternative D $200,000	75 units	3 months	probably infeasible

12. On the basis of the above data, it appears that the one alternative which is dominated by another alternative is Alternative 12.____

A. A B. B C. C D. D

13. If the feasibility constraint is absolute and fixed, then the critical trade-off is between lower cost _______ on the other. 13.____

A. on the one hand and faster timing and higher effectiveness
B. and higher effectiveness on one hand and faster timing
C. and faster timing on the one hand and higher effectiveness
D. on the one hand and higher effectiveness

14. The following illustration depicts the structure of a municipal agency. 14.____

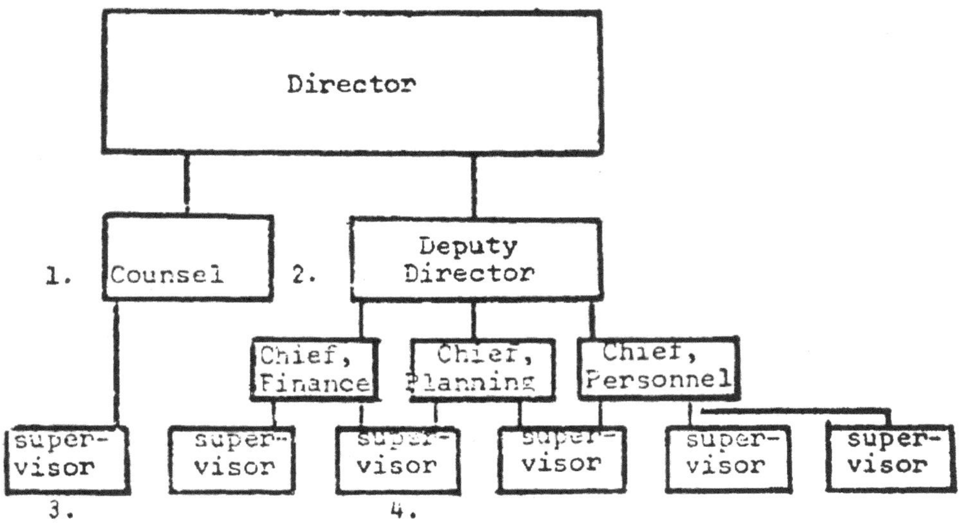

In the above illustration, which individual would generally be expected to encounter the MOST difficulty in carrying out his organizational functions?

A. 1 B. 2 C. 3 D. 4

Questions 15-16.

DIRECTIONS: Questions 15 and 16 are to be answered on the basis of the information given on the report forms pictured below and on the following page.

Chart I and Chart II are parts of the Field Patrol Sheets of two Parking Enforcement Agents. They show the number of violations issued on a particular day. Chart III is the Tally Sheet for that day prepared by the Senior Parking Enforcement Agent from the Field Patrol Sheets of the entire squad.

CHART I

Area or Post	TYPE OF VIOLATION											
	Mtrs	B/S	D/P	Hyd	N/S	N/Sp	Taxi	Curb	N/P	Alt	Other	Total
19	2	3	2	2	3	3	0	1	1	5	1	23
21	4	0	2	0	1	2	2	0	5	9	1	26
Totals	6	3	4	2	4	5	2	1	6	14	2	49

2/4 — Date; 100 — Badge; PEA Browne — Signature

TCB-61 Checked by ____________ Date ______

CHART II

Area or Post	TYPE OF VIOLATION											
	Mtrs	B/S	D/P	Hyd	N/S	N/Sp	Taxi	Curb	N/P	Alt	Other	Total
31	8	2	0	0	3	2	2	0	4	5	0	26
33	7	0	1	2	3	1	2	0	6	3	0	25
Totals	15	2	1	2	6	3	4	0	10	8	0	51

2/4 — Date; 101 — Badge; PEA Grey — Signature

TCB-61 Checked by ____________ Date ______

TRAFFIC CONTROL BUREAU
SENIORS TALLY SHEET

Enf. 23A

Name	Mtrs Ptld	Mtrs	Bus Stop	Dble Park	Hyd	No Stand	No Stop	Taxi Stand	Curb	No Park	Alt Park	Other	Total
Green		18	2	3	1	6	0	0	0	4	10	1	45
Browne		6	3	4	2	4	5	2	1	6	14	2	49
White		12	0	0	0	2	1	1	0	8	8	1	33
Black		20	5	2	3	8	7	5	1	5	4	0	60
Grey		15	2	1	2	9	3	4	0	10	8	0	51
Redding		17	0	1	3	7	5	3	0	8	6	0	50
TOTAL		88	12	11	11	36	21	15	2	41	50	4	288

15. The Senior Parking Enforcement Agent who prepared Chart III made an error in transferring the violation totals from the Field Patrol Sheets to the Seniors Tally Sheet. Which one of the following PROPERLY describes the Tally Sheet entry if this error were corrected? Parking Enforcement Agent 15.____

A. Browne's overall total of summonses issued would be 50
B. Browne's total of summonses issued for Double-Parking violations would be 3
C. Grey's total number of summonses issued for meter violations would be 6
D. Grey's total number of summonses issued for No Standing violations would be 6

16. The parking enforcement agent who issued the MOST summonses for bus stop and taxi stand violations is 16.____

A. Black B. Redding C. White D. Browne

17. During a period of probation in which records were kept for 360 children fourteen to eighteen years of age, probation officers found that the group committed certain offenses, as shown in the following table: 17.____

I.Q.	No. of Offenders	No. of Offenses	Offenses Per Offender
61-80	125	338	2.7
81-100	160	448	2.8
101 & over	75	217	2.9

According to the foregoing data,

A. the more intelligent offenders are no more law-abiding than, and perhaps not so law-abiding as, the dull offenders
B. brighter offenders present no more difficult problems than less intelligent offenders
C. the majority of this probation group is found to be above the average in intelligence of a normal group of young persons within this age range
D. the relationship between the effectiveness of probation work and the number of offenders is in inverse ratio

18. 18.____

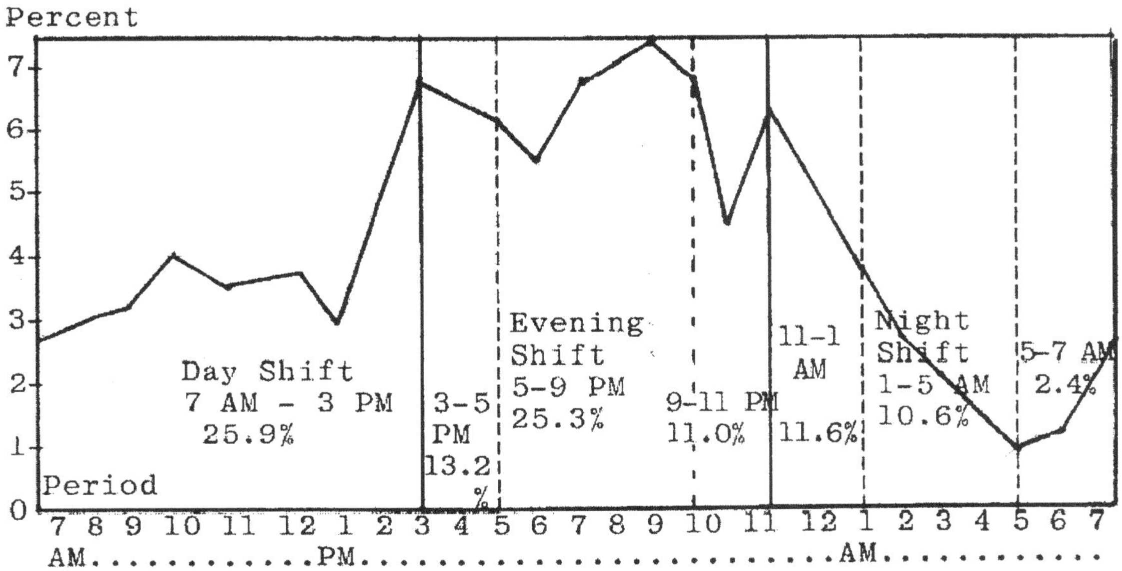

The percent for each hour is charted at the beginning of the hour. For example, 2.6% at the extreme left is for 7:00 A.M. to 7:59 A.M.
A certain police department has analyzed its need for police service and has computed the percentage distributions as shown on the chart on the preceding page. Despite good supervisory effort, there is a significant decrease in the amount of police service provided during the half-hour surrounding shift changes. The police commander wishes to minimize this effect.
To accomplish its objective, taking into account the distribution of need for police services, which one of the following is the BEST time for this department to schedule its three principal shift changes? (Assume 8-hour shifts.)

A. A. 4:00 A.M., Noon, 8:00 P.M.
B. 4:00 A.M., 1:00 P.M., 9:00 P.M.
C. 6:00 A.M., 2:00 P.M., 10:00 P.M.
D. 7:00 A.M., 3:00 P.M., 11:00 P.M.

19. An inspector on a painting contract has to keep records on the progress of the work completed by a painting contractor . 19.____
The following is the progress of the work completed by a contractor at the end of 8 months.

Apartment Size	Estimated Number of Apartments	Number of Apartments Painted
3 rooms	120	100
4 rooms	160	140
5 rooms	120	40

The percentage of work completed on a room basis is MOST NEARLY

A. 62% B. 66% C. 70% D. 74%

20. Assume that an officer reported the following amounts of toll monies collected during each day of a five-day period: 20.____

Tuesday	$3,247.50
Wednesday	$2,992.50
Thursday	$3,917.50
Friday	$4,862.50
Saturday	$1,675.00

The TOTAL amount of toll money collected during this period was

A. $15,702.50 B. $16,485.00
C. $16,695.00 D. $16,997.50

21. Suppose that during a two-hour period in a toll booth an officer collected the following: 21.____

Type of Money	Number of Bills
$20 bills	2
$10 bills	5
$5 bills	23
$1 bills	269

The TOTAL amount of money the officer collected was

A. $299 B. $464 C. $474 D. $501

Questions 22-23.

DIRECTIONS: Questions 22 and 23 are to be answered SOLELY on the basis of the information shown below which indicates the charges for hospital services and physician services given in a hospital and a patient's annual income for each of four consecutive years.

Year	Patient's Annual Income	Charges for Hospital Services and Physician Services Given in a Hospital
2009	$45,000	$11,100
2010	$46,500	$11,970
2011	$64,500	$16,230
2012	$70,500	$17,325

22. A hospitalized patient may qualify for Medicaid benefits when the charges for hospital services and for physician services given in the hospital exceed 25 percent of the patient's annual income. 22.____
According to the information shown above, the one of the following that indicates ONLY those years in which the patient qualifies for Medicaid benefits is

A. 2010, 2011
B. 2009, 2010, 2012
C. 2010, 2012
D. 2010, 2011, 2012

23. The one of the following that is the patient's average annual income for the entire four-year period shown above is MOST NEARLY 23.____

A. $48,375
B. $49,125
C. $56,025
D. $56,625

Questions 24-25.

DIRECTIONS: Questions 24 and 25 are to be answered SOLELY on the basis of the information shown below, which gives the hospital bill and the amount paid by an Insurance Plan for each of four patients.

Patient's Name	Hospital Bill	Amount Paid by the Insurance Plan Toward Hospital Bill
Mr. Harris	$ 8,753	$5,952
Mr. W. Smith	$ 4,504	$3,285
Mr. T. Jones	$ 7,211	$5,048
Mr. M. White	$12,255	$8,712

24. According to the information given above, which patient, when compared with the other three patients, had the HIGHEST percentage of his bill paid by the Insurance Plan? 24.____

A. Mr. W. Smith
B. Mr. D. Harris
C. Mr. T. Jones
D. Mr. M. White

25. The average amount paid by the Insurance Plan toward the hospital bills of the four patients shown above is MOST NEARLY 25.____

A. $5,269
B. $5,499
C. $5,749
D. $5,766

KEY (CORRECT ANSWERS)

1.	D	11.	D
2.	C	12.	C
3.	A	13.	B
4.	B	14.	D
5.	D	15.	D
6.	B	16.	A
7.	A	17.	A
8.	B	18.	C
9.	C	19.	B
10.	A	20.	C

21. C
22. A
23. D
24. A
25. C

TEST 2

DIRECTIONS: Each question or incomplete statement is followed by several suggested answers or completions. Select the one that BEST answers the question or completes the statement. *PRINT THE LETTER OF THE CORRECT ANSWER IN THE SPACE AT THE RIGHT.*

Questions 1-2.

DIRECTIONS: Questions 1 and 2 are to be answered on the basis of the information contained in the chart below.

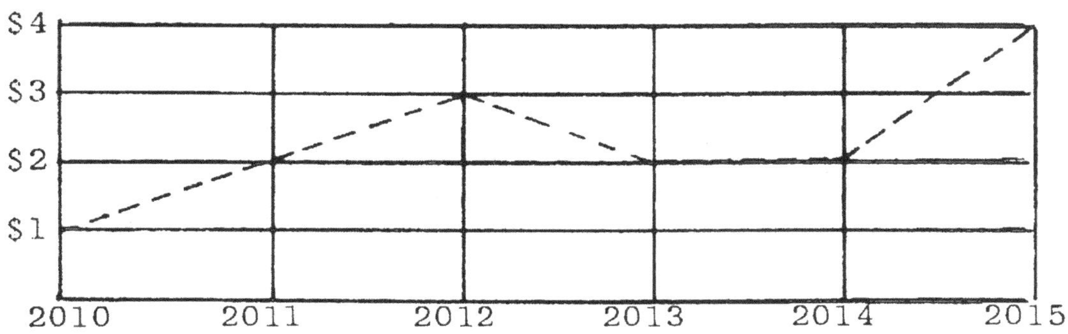

1. According to the above chart, the increase in the average price of the commodity from 2012 to 2015 was APPROXIMATELY 1.____

   A. 25%   B. 33 1/3%   C. 50%   D. 75%

2. According to the above chart, the increase in the average price of the commodity from 2010 to 2012 was APPROXIMATELY 2.____

   A. 20%   B. 30%   C. 200%   D. 300%

Questions 3-4.

DIRECTIONS: Questions 3 and 4 are to be answered SOLELY on the basis of the information contained in the chart below, which shows supply and demand of a commodity from January 1, 2011 to January 1, 2015.

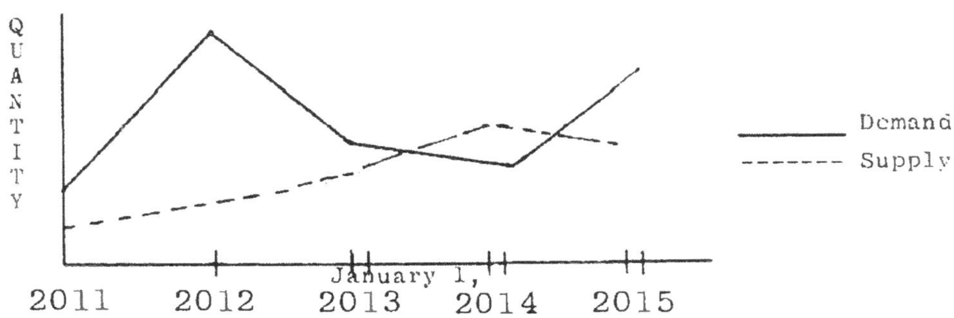

3. The above chart indicates that there was a seller's market during most of each of the following years EXCEPT 3._____

A. 2011 B. 2012 C. 2013 D. 2014

4. According to the above chart, in the absence of price controls or other artificial or unusual circumstances, when would the price of the commodity have been the HIGHEST? 4._____
January 1,

A. 2011 B. 2012 C. 2013 D. 2014

5. In order to pay its employees, the Convex Company obtained bills and coins in the following denominations: 5._____

Denomination	$20	$10	$5	$1	$.50	$.25	$.10	$.05	$.01
Number	317	122	38	73	69	47	39	25	36

What was the TOTAL amount of cash obtained?
A. $7,874.76
B. $7,878.00
C. $7,889.25
D. $7,924.35

6. Suppose that a business you are investigating presents the following figures: 6._____

Year	Net Income	Tax Rate On Net Income
2014	$55,000	20%
2015	$55,000	30%
2016	$65,000	20%
2017	$52,000	25%
2018	$62,000	30%
2019	$68,000	25%

According to these figures, it is MOST accurate to say that
A. less tax was due in 2018 than in 2019
B. more tax was due in 2014 than in 2017
C. the same amount of tax was due in 2014 and 2015
D. the same amount of tax was due in 2016 and 2017

7. The table below shows the total amount of money owed on the bills sent to each of four different accounts and the total amount of money which has been received from each of these accounts. 7._____

Name of Account	Amount Owed	Amount Received
Arnold	$55,989	$37,898
Barry	$97,276	$79,457
Carter	$62,736	$47,769
Daley	$77,463	$59,534

The balance of an account is determined by subtracting the amount received from the amount owed.
Based on this method of determining a balance, the account with the LARGEST balance is
A. Arnold B. Barry C. Carter D. Daley

8. A work sheet for a booth audit has the readings shown below for four turnstiles: 8.____

Turnstile No.	Opening Readings	Readings For Audit
1	26178	26291
2	65489	65752
3	72267	72312
4	45965	46199

With a fare of $1.00, what is the cash value of the TOTAL difference between the Opening Readings and the Readings for Audit for the four turnstiles?

A. $635 B. $653 C. $654 D. $675

Questions 9-10.

DIRECTIONS: Questions 9 and 10 are to be answered SOLELY on the basis of the information contained in the following table.

COMPARISON OF CUNY ATTRITION RATES FOR FALL 2010 DAY FRESHMEN THROUGH FALL 2011

Colleges	Open Admissions (a)	Regular (b)	Overall
Senior	30%	14%	21%
Community	40%	34%	39%
Total	36%	20%	29%

a. Represents senior college students admitted with high school averages below 80 and community college students admitted with high school averages below 75
b. Represents senior college students admitted with averages of 80 and above and community college students admitted with averages of 75 and above

9. The category of students who remained in the City University in the GREATEST proportion were 9.____

A. regular students in community colleges
B. open admissions students in community colleges
C. regular students in senior colleges
D. open admissions students in senior colleges

10. Regular admission to a senior college was on the basis of an academic average 10.____

A. above 70
B. of 80 or above
C. above 75
D. above 85

Questions 11-12.

DIRECTIONS: Questions 11 and 12 are to be answered SOLELY on the basis of the information given below.

Time Scores	
Maximum qualifying time	15 minutes
Minimum qualifying time (subtract)	5 minutes
Range in qualifying time	10 minutes

Weighted Point Scores (Weight = 10)	
Maximum weighted score	10 points
Minimum qualifying score (subtract	7 points
Range in weighted scores	3 points

From the foregoing, it is apparent that a simple conversion table can be prepared by giving the maximum qualifying time a minimum qualifying weighted score of 7 points and crediting three-tenths additional weighted points for each minute less than 15.

11. On the basis of the above paragraph, it is apparent that if the maximum *time* taken by any candidate on the task was 15 minutes, 11.____

  A. the test was too easy
  B. too much weight was given to the *time* portion
  C. less time should have been given for the task
  D. no one failed the *time* portion of the test

12. The BEST of the following interpretations of the above paragraph is that any candidate completing the task in 8 minutes would have received a weighted score for *time* of _______ points. 12.____

  A. 9.1 B. 8.5 C. 8.2 D. 7.9

Questions 13-14.

DIRECTIONS: Questions 13 and 14 are to be answered on the basis of the following illustration. Assume that the figures in the chart are cubes.

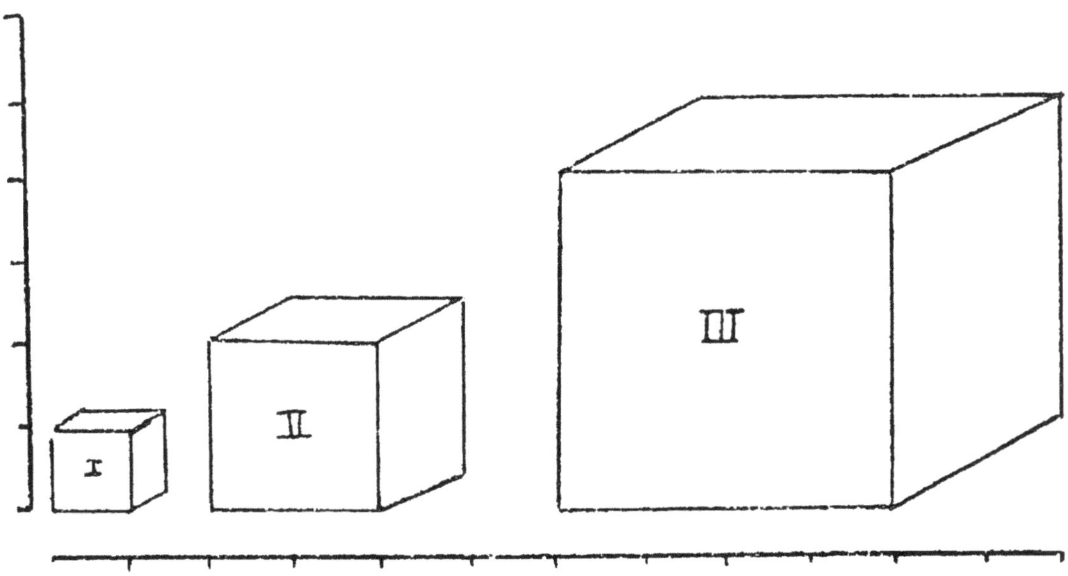

13. In the illustration above, how many times GREATER is the quantity represented by Figure III than the quantity represented by Figure II? 13.____

  A. 2 B. 4 C. 8 D. 16

14. The illustration above illustrates a progression in quantity BEST described as 14.____

A. arithmetic
B. geometric
C. discrete
D. linear

Questions 15-16.

DIRECTIONS: Questions 15 and 16 are to be answered SOLELY on the basis of the following summary of salary increases applicable to a group of employees in a college office.

Hourly Rate 6/30/12	Increase 7/1/12	Increase 7/1/13
$10.20	$1.40/hr.	$1.40/hr.
$11.20	$1.20/hr.	$1.20/hr.
$12.20	$1.20/hr.	$1.20/hr.

Hourly Rate 6/30/12	Increase 7/1/12	Increase 7/1/13
$13.20	$1.00/hr.	$1.00/hr.
$14.20	$1.00/hr.	$1.00/hr.
$15.20	$1.00/hr.	$1.00/hr.

15. A college office employee with an hourly salary of $14.20 as of June 30, 2012 worked for 32 hours during the week of April 16, 2013. 15.____
Her GROSS salary for that week was

A. $422.40 B. $454.40 C. $486.40 D. $518.40

16. A college office employee was earning an hourly salary of $12.20 in June of 2012. 16.____
The percentage increase in her hourly salary as of July 2, 2013 will be MOST NEARLY _______ percent.

A. 10 B. 15 C. 20 D. 25

17. An experiment was conducted to measure the error rate of typists. The results follow: 17.____

Typists	Percent of Total Output	Error Rate (in percent)
A	30	1.00
B	30	1.50
C	40	0.50

The error rate (in percent) for the three typists combined
A. is 0.95
B. is 1.00
C. is 3.00
D. cannot be calculated from the given data

Question 18.

DIRECTIONS: Question 18 is to be answered on the basis of the information given below.

At midnight on January 31, the following bodies were remaining:

Adults	Infants	Stillbirths	Amputations
37	23	40	21

On February 1st, from 12:01 A.M. to 12:00 midnight, the following bodies were received:

Adults	Infants	Stillbirths	Amputations
24	13	18	8

In addition, the following bodies were claimed:

Adults	Infants	Stillbirths	Amputations
33	9	4	2

18. What is the number of cases remaining at midnight on February 1? 18.____

	Adults	Infants	Stillbirths	Amputations
A.	31	26	41	23
B.	28	27	54	27
C.	29	28	48	25
D.	27	29	62	28

Questions 19-25.

DIRECTIONS: Questions 19 through 25 are to be answered SOLELY on the basis of the following information.

ACCIDENTS

During one month, a certain division reported the number of accidents from various causes as follows:

Falls	6
Flying objects....................................	5
Handling objects	4
Striking objects	3
Assaults	2
Stepping on objects	1

19. The GREATEST cause of accidents was 19.____

A. striking objects
B. handling objects
C. flying objects
D. falls

20. The accidents over which the injured person had LEAST control were those due to 20.____

A. handling objects
B. falls
C. assaults
D. flying objects

21. The accidents due to flying objects exceeded those due to striking objects by 21.____

A. 8 B. 6 C. 3 D. 2

22. The TOTAL number of accidents as shown was 22.____

A. 19 B. 20 C. 21 D. 22

23. The MOST likely cause for an accident to a station porter is 23.____

A. stepping on objects
B. falls
C. striking objects
D. assaults

24. The accidents which would MOST likely result in disciplinary action are those due to 24.____

A. stepping on objects
B. assaults
C. striking objects
D. falls

25. The TOTAL number of accidents involving objects was 25.____

A. 8 B. 12 C. 13 D. 21

KEY (CORRECT ANSWERS)

1.	B	11.	D
2.	C	12.	A
3.	C	13.	C
4.	B	14.	B
5.	A	15.	C
6.	D	16.	C
7.	A	17.	A
8.	C	18.	B
9.	C	19.	D
10.	B	20.	D

21. D
22. C
23. B
24. B
25. C

PREPARING WRITTEN MATERIAL

PARAGRAPH REARRANGEMENT COMMENTARY

The sentences which follow are in scrambled order. You are to rearrange them in proper order and indicate the letter choice containing the correct answer at the space at the right.

Each group of sentences in this section is actually a paragraph presented in scrambled order. Each sentence in the group has a place in that paragraph; no sentence is to be left out. You are to read each group of sentences and decide upon the best order in which to put the sentences so as to form as well-organized paragraph.

The questions in this section measure the ability to solve a problem when all the facts relevant to its solution are not given.

More specifically, certain positions of responsibility and authority require the employee to discover connections between events sometimes, apparently, unrelated. In order to do this, the employee will find it necessary to correctly infer that unspecified events have probably occurred or are likely to occur. This ability becomes especially important when action must be taken on incomplete information.

Accordingly, these questions require competitors to choose among several suggested alternatives, each of which presents a different sequential arrangement of the events. Competitors must choose the MOST logical of the suggested sequences.

In order to do so, they may be required to draw on general knowledge to infer missing concepts or events that are essential to sequencing the given events. Competitors should be careful to infer only what is essential to the sequence. The plausibility of the wrong alternatives will always require the inclusion of unlikely events or of additional chains of events which are NOT essential to sequencing the given events.

It's very important to remember that you are looking for the best of the four possible choices, and that the best choice of all may not even be one of the answers you're given to choose from.

There is no one right way to solve these problems. Many people have found it helpful to first write out the order of the sentences, as they would have arranged them, on their scrap paper before looking at the possible answers. If their optimum answer is there, this can save them some time. If it isn't, this method can still give insight into solving the problem. Others find it most helpful to just go through each of the possible choices, contrasting each as they go along. You should use whatever method feels comfortable, and works, for you.

While most of these types of questions are not that difficult, we've added a higher percentage of the difficult type, just to give you more practice. Usually there are only one or two questions on this section that contain such subtle distinctions that you're unable to answer confidently, and you then may find yourself stuck deciding between two possible choices, neither of which you're sure about.

EXAMINATION SECTION

TEST 1

DIRECTIONS: The sentences that follow are in scrambled order. You are to rearrange them in proper order and indicate the letter choice containing the correct answer. *PRINT THE LETTER OF THE CORRECT ANSWER IN THE SPACE AT THE RIGHT.*

1. Below are four statements labeled W, X, Y and Z. 1.____
   W. He was a strict and fanatic drillmaster.
   X. The word is always used in a derogatory sense and generally shows resentment and anger on the part of the user.
   Y. It is from the name of this Frenchman that we derive our English word, martinet.
   Z. Jean Martinet was the Inspector-General of Infantry during the reign of King Louis XIV.
   The PROPER order in which these sentences should be placed in a paragraph is:
   A. X, Z, W, Y B. X, Z, Y, W C. Z, W, Y, X D. Z, Y, W, X

2. In the following paragraph, the sentences, which are numbered, have been jumbled. 2.____
   I. Since then it has undergone changes.
   II. It was incorporated in 1955 under the laws of the State of New York.
   III. Its primary purposes, a cleaner city, has, however, remained the same.
   IV. The Citizens Committee works in cooperation with the Mayor's Inter-departmental Committee for a Clean City. 3.____
   The order in which these sentences should be arranged to form a well-organized paragraph is:
   A. II, IV, I, III B. III, IV, I, II C. IV, II, I, III D. IV, III, II, I

Questions 3-5.

DIRECTIONS: The sentences listed below are part of a meaningful paragraph but they are not given in their proper order. You are to decide what would be the BEST order in which to put the sentences so as to form a well-organized paragraph. Each sentence has a place in the paragraph; there are no extra sentences. You are then to answer Questions 3 through 5 inclusive on the basis of your rearrangements of these scrambled sentences into a properly organized paragraph.

In 1887 some insurance companies organized an Inspection Department to advise their clients on all phases of fire prevention and protection. Probably this has been due to the smaller annual fire losses in Great Britain than in the United States. It tests various fire prevention devices and appliances and determines manufacturing hazards and their safeguards. Fire research began earlier in the United States and is more advanced than in Great Britain. Later they established a laboratory specializing in electrical, mechanical, hydraulic, and chemical fields.

3. When the five sentences are arranged in proper order, the paragraph starts with the sentence which begins 3.____
   A. "In 1887..." B. "Probably this..." C. "It tests..."
   D. "Fire research..." E. "Later they..."

4. In the last sentence listed above, "they" refers to 4.____
   A. the insurance companies B. the United States and Great Britain
   C. the Inspection Department D. clients
   E. technicians

5. When the above paragraph is properly arranged, it ends with the words 5.____
   A. "...and protection." B. "...the United States."
   C. "...their safeguards." D. "...in Great Britain."
   E. "...chemical fields."

KEY (CORRECT ANSWERS)

1. C
2. C
3. D
4. A
5. C

TEST 2

DIRECTIONS: In each of the questions numbered I through V, several sentences are given. For each question, choose as your answer the group of number that represents the MOST logical order of these sentences if they were arranged in paragraph form. *PRINT THE LETTER OF THE CORRECT ANSWER IN THE SPACE AT THE RIGHT.*

1. I. It is established when one shows that the landlord has prevented the tenant's enjoyment of his interest in the property leased. 1.____
   II. Constructive eviction is the result of a breach of the covenant of quiet enjoyment implied in all leases.
   III. In some parts of the United States, it is not complete until the tenant vacates within a reasonable time.
   IV. Generally, the acts must be of such serious and permanent character as to deny the tenant the enjoyment of his possessing rights.
   V. In this event, upon abandonment of the premises, the tenant's liability for that ceases.

   The CORRECT answer is:
   A. II, I, IV, III, V
   B. V, II, III, I, IV
   C. IV, III, I, II, V
   D. I, III, V, IV, II

2. I. The powerlessness before private and public authorities that is the typical experience of the slum tenant is reminiscent of the situation of blue-collar workers all through the nineteenth century. 2.____
   II. Similarly, in recent years, this chapter of history has been reopened by anti-poverty groups which have attempted to organize slum tenants to enable them to bargain collectively with their landlords about the conditions of their tenancies.
   III. It is familiar history that many of the worker remedied their condition by joining together and presenting their demands collectively.
   IV. Like the workers, tenants are forced by the conditions of modern life into substantial dependence on these who possess great political aid and economic power.
   V. What's more, the very fact of dependence coupled with an absence of education and self-confidence makes them hesitant and unable to stand up for what they need from those in power.

   The CORRECT answer is:
   A. V, IV, I, II, III
   B. II, III, I, V, IV
   C. III, I, V, IV, II
   D. I, IV, V, III, II

3. I. A railroad, for example, when not acting as a common carrier may contract away responsibility for its own negligence. 3.____
   II. As to a landlord, however, no decision has been found relating to the legal effect of a clause shifting the statutory duty of repair to the tenant.
   III. The courts have not passed on the validity of clauses relieving the landlord of this duty and liability.
   IV. They have, however, upheld the validity of exculpatory clauses in other types of contracts.

V. Housing regulations impose a duty upon the landlord to maintain leased premises in safe condition.
VI. As another example, a bailee may limit his liability except for gross negligence, willful acts, or fraud.

The CORRECT answer is:

A. II, I, VI, IV, III, V
B. I, III, IV, V, VI, II
C. III, V, I, IV, II, VI
D. V, III, IV, I, VI, II

4. I. Since there are only samples in the building, retail or consumer sales are generally eschewed by mart occupants, and in some instances, rigid controls are maintained to limit entrance to the mart only to those persons engaged in retailing. 4.____
II. Since World War I, in many larger cities, there has developed a new type of property, called the mart building.
III. It can, therefore, be used by wholesalers and jobbers for the display of sample merchandise.
IV. This type of building is most frequently a multi-storied, finished interior property which is a cross between a retail arcade and a loft building.
V. This limitation enables the mart occupants to ship the orders from another location after the retailer or dealer makes his selection from the samples.

The CORRECT answer is:

A. II, IV, III, I, V
B. IV, III, V, I, II
C. I, III, II, IV, V
D. I, IV, I, III, V

5. I. In general, staff-line friction reduces the distinctive contribution of staff personnel. 5.____
II. The conflicts, however, introduce an uncontrolled element into the managerial system.
III. On the other hand, the natural resistance of the line to staff innovations probably usefully restrains over-eager efforts to apply untested procedures on a large scale.
IV. Under such conditions, it is difficult to know when valuable ideas are being sacrificed.
V. The relatively weak position of staff, requiring accommodation to the line, tends to restrict their ability to engage in free, experimental innovation.

The CORRECT answer is:

A. IV, II, III, I, V
B. I, V, III, II, IV
C. V, III, I, II, IV
D. II, I, IV, V, III

KEY (CORRECT ANSWERS)

1. A
2. D
3. D
4. A
5. B

TEST 3

DIRECTIONS: Questions 1 through 4 consist of six sentences which can be arranged in a logical sequence. For each question, select the choice which places the numbered sentences in the MOST logical sequent. *PRINT THE LETTER OF THE CORRECT ANSWER IN THE SPACE AT THE RIGHT.*

1. I. The burden of proof as to each issue is determined before trial and remains upon the same party throughout the trial. 1.____
   II. The jury is at liberty to believe one witness' testimony as against a number of contradictory witnesses.
   III. In a civil case, the party bearing the burden of proof is required to prove his contention by a fair preponderance of the evidence.
   IV. However, it must be noted that a fair preponderance of evidence does not necessarily mean a greater number of witnesses.
   V. The burden of proof is the burden which rests upon one of the parties to an action to persuade the trier of the facts, generally the jury, that a proposition he asserts is true.
   VI. If the evidence is equally balanced, or if it leaves the jury in such doubt as to be unable to decide the controversy either way, judgment must be given against the party upon whom the burden of proof rests.

   The CORRECT answer is:
   A. III, II, V, IV, I, VI
   B. I, II, VI, V, III, IV
   C. III, IV, V, I, II, VI
   D. V, I, III, VI, IV, II

2. I. If a parent is without assets and is unemployed, he cannot be convicted of the crime of non-support of a child. 2.____
   II. The term "sufficient ability" has been held to mean sufficient financial ability.
   III. It does not matter if his unemployment is by choice or unavoidable circumstances.
   IV. If he fails to take any steps at all, he may be liable to prosecution for endangering the welfare of a child.
   V. Under the penal law, a parent is responsible for the support of his minor child only if the parent is "of sufficient ability."
   VI. An indigent parent may meet his obligation by borrowing money or by seeking aid under the provisions of the Social Welfare Law.

   The CORRECT answer is:
   A. VI, I, V, III, II, IV
   B. I, III, V, II, IV, VI
   C. V, II, I, III, VI, IV
   D. I, VI, IV, V, II, III

3. I. Consider, for example, the case of a rabble rouser who urges a group of twenty people to go out and break the windows of a nearby factory. 3.____
   II. Therefore, the law fills the indicated gap with the crime of inciting to riot.
   III. A person is considered guilty of inciting to riot when he urges ten or more persons to engage in tumultuous and violent conduct of a kind likely to create public alarm.
   IV. However, if he has not obtained the cooperation of at least four people, he cannot be charged with unlawful assembly.

V. The charge of inciting to riot was added to the law to cover types of conduct which cannot be classified as either the crime of "riot" or the crime of "unlawful assembly."
VI. If he acquires the acquiescence of at least four of them, he is guilty of unlawful assembly even if the project does not materialize.

The CORRECT answer is:

A. III, V, I, VI, IV, II
B. V, I, IV, VI, II, III
C. III, IV, I, V, II, VI
D. V, I, IV, VI, III, II

4. I. If, however, the rebuttal evidence presents an issue of credibility, it is for the jury to determine whether the presumption has, in fact, been destroyed. 4.____
II. Once sufficient evidence to the contrary is introduced, the presumption disappears from the trial.
III. The effect of a presumption is to place the burden upon the adversary to come forward with evidence to rebut the presumption.
IV. When a presumption is overcome and ceases to exist in the case, the fact or facts which gave rise to the presumption still remain.
V. Whether a presumption has been overcome is ordinarily a question for the court.
VI. Such information may furnish a basis for a logical inference.

The CORRECT answer is:

A. IV, VI, II, V, I, III
B. III, II, V, I, IV, VI
C. V, III, VI, IV, II, I
D. V, IV, I, II, VI, III

KEY (CORRECT ANSWERS)

1. D
2. C
3. A
4. B

EXAMINATION SECTION
TEST 1

DIRECTIONS: Each question or incomplete statement is followed by several suggested answers or completions. Select the one that BEST answers the question or completes the statement. *PRINT THE LETTER OF THE CORRECT ANSWER IN THE SPACE AT THE RIGHT.*

Questions 1-4.

DIRECTIONS: Questions 1 through 4 are to be answered on the basis of the following passage.

A State department which is interested in finding acceptable solutions to the operational problems of specific types of community self-help organizations recently sent two of its staff members to meet with one such organization. At that meeting, the leaders of the community organization voiced the need for increased activity planning input of a more detailed nature from the citizens regularly served by that organization. There followed a discussion of a number of information-gathering methods, including surveys by telephone, questionnaires mailed to the citizens' residences, in-person interviews with the citizens, and the placing of suggestion boxes in the organization's headquarters building. Concern was expressed by one of the leaders that the organization's funds be spent judiciously. The State department representatives present promised to investigate the possibility of a matching fund grant of money to the organization.

Later, the proposed survey was conducted using questionnaires completed by those citizens who visited the organization's headquarters. The results of the survey included the information that twice as many citizens wanted more educational activities scheduled than wanted more social activities scheduled, whereas one-half of those who wanted more educational activities scheduled were interested mainly in special job training.

1. A similar survey conducted by a State department employee involved special job training. That survey uncovered the information below. The following four sentences are to be rearranged to form the most effective and logical paragraph. Select the letter representing the best sequence for these sentences. 1._____

    I. The majority of those who are still in this group are ethnic minorities.
    II. The number of economically disadvantaged people who enjoyed their special job training is larger than the number of economically disadvantaged people who did not enjoy it.
    III. Thirty-five percent of all those who are economically disadvantaged are not ethnic minorities.
    IV. Eighty percent of those who have completed special job training in the past ten years are economically disadvantaged.

    The CORRECT answer is:

    A. IV, I, III, II
    B. I, III, II, IV
    C. IV, II, I. III
    D. I, II, III, IV

2. In the reading passage above, the word *judiciously* means MOST NEARLY 2._____

    A. legally
    B. immediately
    C. prudently
    D. uniformly

3. Based *only* on the information in the reading passage, which one of the following statements is MOST fully supported? 3.____

   A. The leaders of the community organization in question wanted to increase the quantity and quality of feedback about that organization's suggestion boxes.
   B. The number of citizens surveyed who wanted more educational activities scheduled and were mainly interested in special job training was the same as the number of citizens surveyed who wanted more social activities to be scheduled.
   C. At the meeting concerned, matching funds were promised to the community organization in question by the two State department representatives present.
   D. Telephone surveys generally yield more accurate information than do surveys conducted through the use of mailed questionnaires.

4. The following four sentences are to be rearranged to form the most effective and logical paragraph. Select the letter representing the best sequence for these sentences. 4.____

   I. Formal surveys of citizens within a community also convey to those citizens the interest of the community leadership in hearing the citizens' ideas about community improvement.
   II. Such surveys can provide needed input into the process of establishing specific community program goals.
   III. Formally conducted surveys of community residents often yield valuable information to the local area leaders responsible for community-based programs.
   IV. No community should formulate these goals without attempting to obtain the views of its citizenry.

   The CORRECT answer is:

   A. III, I, IV, II
   B. I, III, II, IV
   C. III, II, IV, I
   D. IV, III, II, I

Questions 5-8.

DIRECTIONS: Questions 5 through 8 are to be answered on the basis of the following passage.

The Smith Paint Company, which currently employs 2,000 persons, has been in existence for 20 years. A new chemical paint, Futuron, was recently developed by an employee of that company. This paint was released for public use a month ago on a trial basis. The sales were phenomenal, and there is a great demand for more Futuron to be manufactured. The profits to be made by increased manufacturing and sale of Futuron could place the Smith Paint Company in a leading role in the paint industry.

The Smith Paint Company currently produces 2 million gallons of the more traditional paint per year. The Smith Paint Company's Board of Directors wishes to reduce its production of this traditional paint by 50%, and to produce 1 million gallons of Futuron per year.

The employees are quite concerned about this potential production change. A public nonprofit research group has been investigating the chemical make-up of Futuron. Initial research indicates that negative physical reactions may result from working closely with the chemicals necessary to manufacture Futuron. For this reason, most of the company employees do not want the proposed change in production to occur. The members of the Board of Directors, however, argue that the research results are too inconclusive to cause great concern. They say that the company would lose 25% to 50% of its potential profit if the large-scale manufacturing of Futuron is not initiated immediately.

5. Seventy-five percent of the Smith Paint Company's current employees were hired during its first 10 years of operation. Fifteen percent were hired in the past five years. During the five-year interval between the first ten years and the most recent five years, 40 persons were hired per year. 5._____
What percentage of its total employees were hired during the Smith Paint Company's first 13 years of operation?

   A. 75% B. 81% C. 85% D. 90%

6. Assume that the total possible profit the Smith Paint Company could make during its first year of manufacturing the proposed amount of Futuron would be $1.00 per gallon. The purchase of new machinery would reduce this first-year profit by 50%. The anticipated delay, during the first production year, in establishing large-scale manufacturing facilities would reduce the total possible profit by an additional 25%. 6._____
Given this information, what would be the actual profit made from the first year of manufacturing Futuron?

   A. $250,000 B. $375,000 C. $500,000 D. $750,000

7. In the reading passage, the word *inconclusive* means MOST NEARLY 7._____

   A. ineluctable B. incorrect
   C. unreasonable D. indeterminate

8. Based on the information in the reading passage, which of the following statements represents the MOST accurate conclusion? 8._____

   A. The proposed reduction in the production of its traditional paint would not financially injure the Smith Paint Company.
   B. A greater proportion of the Smith Paint Company's employees are in favor of the proposed increase in Futuron production than are opposed to it.
   C. The increased Futuron production proposed by the Smith Paint Company's Board of Directors would cause that company's employees considerable health damage.
   D. Positive public response to the sale of Futuron suggests that considerable profit can be made by increasing the manufacturing and sale of Futuron.

KEY (CORRECT ANSWERS)

1. A
2. C
3. B
4. C
5. B
6. A
7. D
8. D

SOLUTIONS TO PROBLEMS

1. For the following reasons, Choice A is correct and the other three choices are incorrect:

    1. Both Choice B and Choice D begin with Sentence I, which states, *The majority of those who are still in this group are ethnic minorities.* The paragraph cannot logically begin with a statement such as Sentence I, because no one reading the paragraph would know what *this group* refers to. Therefore, Choice B and Choice D are not correct and may be eliminated from consideration.

    2. Both Choice A and Choice C begin with Sentence IV, which states, *Eighty percent of those who have completed special job training in the past ten years are economically disadvantaged.* The problem then becomes selecting the best sequence of the other three sentences so that they most logically follow the initial Sentence IV.

    3. If you select Choice C, then you are choosing Sentence II as the correct second sentence. Sentence II states, *The number of economically disadvantaged people who enjoyed their special job training is larger than the number of economically disadvantaged people who did not enjoy it.* Then Sentence I would be the third sentence. However, that would not be logical, because you could not tell whether *this group* in Sentence I refers to *economically disadvantaged people who enjoyed their special job training* or whether *this group* refers to *economically disadvantaged people who did not enjoy it.* Therefore, Choice C is not correct.

    4. By the process of elimination, only Choice A remains. Choice A specifies Sentence I as the second sentence, which is logically correct in that *this group* in Sentence I will then refer to those who *are economically disadvantaged* in Sentence IV. The two remaining sentences also refer back to *economically disadvantaged,* thus creating a paragraph that reads logically from start to finish. Therefore, Choice A is the correct answer.

2. Choices B and D should be eliminated from further consideration due to the context in which the word *judiciously* was used in the reading passage. Specifically, concern was expressed that funds be spent judiciously. Nothing in the paragraph suggests a need for concern if the funds were not spent immediately or uniformly. Choice A must be considered, because public funds should be spent legally. However, the word *judiciously* is related to the word *judgment* rather than to the word *judiciary.* It is the latter word that has to do with courts of law and is related to legality, so Choice A is incorrect. On the other hand, *judiciously* and *prudently* both mean *wisely* and *with direction.* Therefore, Choice C is correct.

3. Choice B is the correct choice. No matter what numbers you apply, Choice B still will be correct. This is because when you multiply any number by two and then divide the result in half, you end up with the same number that you began with. For example, suppose that 20 citizens wanted more social activities. Twice that number (40 citizens) wanted more educational activities. But of those 40 citizens, one-half (20 citizens) wanted mainly special job training.

Choice A is incorrect because, first of all, the organization did not have any suggestion boxes; although suggestion boxes were discussed, questionnaires ultimately were used instead. In addition, Choice A is incorrect because it was input about the planning of activities that the leaders of the community organization wanted rather than feedback concerning suggestion boxes.

Choice C also is not correct. Instead of promising the matching funds, the State department representatives promised to investigate (or look into) the possibility of obtaining the matching funds.

Choice D is incorrect because the reading passage does not tell whether telephone surveys or mailed questionnaires provide more accurate information. Remember, the instructions for this question state that the question is to be answered based ONLY on the information in the applicable reading passage.

4. The correct answer is Choice C. Choice A and Choice C both begin with Sentence III, which certainly could be the logical first sentence of a paragraph. However, the next sentence (Sentence I) in Choice A leaves the initial topic of obtaining information from citizens. The third sentence in Choice A would be Sentence IV, *No community should formulate these goals without attempting to obtain the views of its citizenry.* The words *these goals* do not logically refer to anything in the previous two sentences, so Choice A is incorrect.

   Choice B also is incorrect because the word *also* in its first sentence (Sentence I) has nothing to logically refer to. *Also* would have to be used in a sentence that comes later in the paragraph.

   Choice D has the same problem as Choice A. Choice D begins with Sentence IV, which starts off, *No community should formulate these goals....* Again, the words *these goals* need to refer to something in a previous sentence about goals in order to be logically correct.

5. Choice B is correct. Here are the mathematical computations you might use to arrive at the correct answer of 81%:

   1. The reading passage states that the Smith Paint Company currently employs 2,000 persons. The first part of this question states that 75% of those current employees were hired during the first ten years that the company was in operation. By multiplying 75% by 2,000, you would find that 1,500 of the current employees were hired during the company's first ten years.

   2. The question asks about the first 13 years of the company's operation rather than just the first ten years. Therefore, you need the arithmetical information for the three years that immediately followed the first ten years. You know from the reading passage that the company has been operating for 20 years. You have the information for the first ten years. Twenty minus ten leaves the most recent ten years.

3. You know from the question that 40 persons were hired each year during the five-year period of time between the first ten years and the most recent five years. However, you need information about only the first three years. By multiplying 40 persons per year by three years, you would find that 120 people were hired during the first three years that came immediately after the first ten years of the company's operation.

4. Next, you would need to add 1,500 people (for the first ten years) and 120 people (for the next three years). That would give you a total of 1,620 people hired during the first 13 years.

5. The question asks for the percentage of the Smith Paint Company's total employees hired during its first 13 years. You know that the total number of employees is 2,000.The question then is: 1,620 people is what percentage of 2,000 people? By dividing 2,000 into 1,620, you would find that the correct answer is 81%.

Choice A is incorrect because it deals with only the first ten years that the company was in operation, rather than the first 13 years. If you took 1,500 people (from Step 1 in the explanatory material for the correct answer) and divided that number by 2,000 people, you would arrive at 75%, which is not correct.

Choice C is incorrect. If you correctly arrived at 1,500 people for the first ten years but then incorrectly dealt with the next five years instead of the next three years, you would end up with the wrong answer of 85%. First, you would multiply 40 people by five years and end up with 200 people. Next, you would add 200 to 1,500 and end up with 1,700 people. Finally, you would divide 1,700 by 2,000 and get 85%.

Choice D also is incorrect. If you correctly arrived at 1,500 people for the first ten years but then used the information for the most recent five years instead of the information for the five years that came just before the most recent five years, you would end up with the incorrect answer of 90%. First, you would find from the question that 15% of the total employees were hired in the past five years. Next, you would multiply 15% by 2,000 total employees and end up with 300. Next, you would add 1,500 employees and 300 employees, ending up with a total of 1,800 employees. By dividing 1,800 by 2,000, you would arrive at 90%.

6. Choice A is correct. Here are the mathematical computations you would need to make to arrive at the correct answer of $250,000:

   1. The reading passage states that the amount of Futuron proposed for manufacture each year is 1 million gallons. The question states that the possible profit per gallon would be $1.00. By multiplying $1.00 by 1,000,000, you would find that $1,000,000 would be the total possible profit to be made during the first year.

   2. The question states that the $1,000,000 possible profit would have to be reduced by 50% because of the purchase of new machinery, plus by an additional 25% due to the delay in establishing manufacturing facilities. The possible profit must, therefore, be reduced by 50% plus 25%, or by a total of 75%, leaving only 25% of the $1,000,000 as possible profit.

3. By multiplying 25% by $1,000,000, you would arrive at $250,000 as the actual profit which would be made.

Choice B is incorrect. If the two profit reductions were incorrectly multiplied by one another (50% times 25%) and the product (12 1/2%) added to 50%, there would have been a net reduction of 62 1/2%, yielding $375,000. However, the two profit reductions are independent of each other and should be added together.

Choice C also is incorrect. It would occur if you only took into account the 50% profit reduction. However, as the paragraph states, you must also deduct an additional 25% of the total profit.

Choice D ($750,000) would be made if you incorrectly multiplied the total profit reduction (75%) by $1,000,000. However, the question asks for the profit, not the profit reduction.

7. Both *indeterminate* and *inconclusive* mean *vague* and *indefinite,* so Choice D is correct. Choice A is incorrect, because the word *ineluctable* means inescapable or inevitable. The reading passage does not support the conclusion that the research results are incorrect or unreasonable, so Choice B and Choice C can be eliminated from consideration.

8. Choice D is correct. The reading passage states, *The sales were phenomenal, and there is a great demand for more Futuron to be manufactured. The profits to be made by increasing the manufacturing and sale of Futuron could place the Smith Paint Company in a leading role in the paint industry.* Since the sales of Futuron were phenomenal (remarkable; extraordinary), and there still is a great demand for it, the suggestion of considerable future profit is reasonable.

   Choice A is not the most accurate conclusion based on the reading passage. The financial impact of decreasing the production of the traditional paint cannot be ascertained. Therefore, it is not certain that the proposed 50% reduction in the manufacturing of the Smith Paint Company's traditional paint would not financially injure that company. Certainly, Choice D is a more accurate conclusion.

   Choice B is incorrect. A greater proportion of the employees being in favor of the proposed increase in Futuron production than not being in favor of it implies that over 50% of the employees are in favor of it. However, the reading passage states that most of the employees (which, logically, means over 50% of the employees) do not want the proposed change to occur.

   Choice C also is not the most accurate conclusion. It states that the proposed increase in Futuron production would cause employees considerable health damage. The reading passage is not definite on this issue of health damage. It states, *Initial research indicates that negative physical reactions may result from working closely with the chemicals necessary....* How serious the health damage might be is not stated in the reading passage.

PREPARING WRITTEN MATERIALS

EXAMINATION SECTION
TEST 1

DIRECTIONS: Each question consists of a sentence which may be classified appropriately under one of the following four categories:

A. Incorrect because of faulty grammar or sentence structure;
B. Incorrect because of faulty punctuation;
C. Incorrect because of faulty capitalization;
D. Correct.

Examine each sentence carefully. Then, in the space at the right, indicate the letter preceding the category which is the BEST of the four suggested above. Each incorrect sentence contains only one type of error. Consider a sentence correct if it contains no errors, although there may be other correct ways of expressing the same thought.

1. All the employees, in this office, are over twenty-one years old. 1.____

2. Neither the clerk nor the stenographer was able to explain what had happened. 2.____

3. Mr. Johnson did not know who he would assign to type the order. 3.____

4. Mr. Marshall called her to report for work on saturday. 4.____

5. He might of arrived on time if the train had not been delayed. 5.____

6. Some employees on the other hand, are required to fill out these forms every month. 6.____

7. The supervisor issued special instructions to his subordinates to prevent their making errors. 7.____

8. Our supervisor Mr. Williams, expects to be promoted in about two weeks. 8.____

9. We were informed that prof. Morgan would attend the conference. 9.____

10. The clerks were assigned to the old building; the stenographers, to the new building. 10.____

11. The supervisor asked Mr. Smith and I to complete the work as quickly as possible. 11.____

12. He said, that before an employee can be permitted to leave, the report must be finished. 12.____

13. An adding machine, in addition to the three typewriters, are needed in the new office. 13.____

14. Having made many errors in her work, the supervisor asked the typist to be more careful. 14.____

15. "If you are given an assignment," he said, "you should begin work on it as quickly as possible." 15.____

16. All the clerks, including those who have been appointed recently are required to work on the new assignment. 16.____

17. The office manager asked each employee to work one saturday a month. 17.____

18. Neither Mr. Smith nor Mr. Jones was able to finish his assignment on time. 18.____

19. The task of filing these cards is to be divided equally between you and he. 19.____

20. He is an employee whom we consider to be efficient. 20.____

21. I believe that the new employees are not as punctual as us. 21.____

22. The employees, working in this office, are to be congratulated for their work. 22.____

23. The delay in preparing the report was caused, in his opinion, by the lack of proper supervision and coordination. 23.____

24. John Jones accidentally pushed the wrong button and then all the lights went out. 24.____

25. The investigator ought to of had the witness sign the statement. 25.____

KEY (CORRECT ANSWERS)

1.	B	11.	A
2.	D	12.	B
3.	A	13.	A
4.	C	14.	A
5.	A	15.	D
6.	B	16.	B
7.	D	17.	C
8.	B	18.	D
9.	C	19.	A
10.	D	20.	D

21. A
22. B
23. D
24. D
25. A

TEST 2

Questions 1-10.

DIRECTIONS: Each of the following sentences may be classified under one of the following four options:

A. Faulty; contains an error in grammar only
B. Faulty; contains an error in spelling only
C. Faulty; contains an error in grammar and an error in spelling
D. Correct; contains no error in grammar or in spelling

Examine each sentence carefully to determine under which of the above four options it is BEST classified. Then, in the space at the right, write the letter preceding the option which is the best of the four listed above.

1. A recognized principle of good management is that an assignment should be given to whomever is best qualified to carry it out. 1.____

2. He considered it a privilege to be allowed to review and summarize the technical reports issued annually by your agency. 2.____

3. Because the warehouse was in an inaccessable location, deliveries of electric fixtures from the warehouse were made only in large lots. 3.____

4. Having requisitioned the office supplies, Miss Brown returned to her desk and resumed the computation of petty cash disbursements. 4.____

5. One of the advantages of this chemical solution is that records treated with it are not inflamable. 5.____

6. The complaint of this employee, in addition to the complaints of the other employees, were submitted to the grievance committee. 6.____

7. A study of the duties and responsibilities of each of the various categories of employees was conducted by an unprejudiced classification analyst. 7.____

8. Ties of friendship with this subordinate compels him to withold the censure that the subordinate deserves. 8.____

9. Neither of the agencies are affected by the decision to institute a program for rehabilitating physically handi-caped men and women. 9.____

10. The chairman stated that the argument between you and he was creating an intolerable situation. 10.____

Questions 11-25.

DIRECTIONS: Each of the following sentences may be classified under one of the following four options:

A. Correct
B. Sentence contains an error in spelling
C. Sentence contains an error in grammar
D. Sentence contains errors in both grammar and spelling.

11. He reported that he had had a really good time during his vacation although the farm was located in a very inaccessible portion of the country. 11.____

12. It looks to me like he has been fasinated by that beautiful painting. 12.____

13. We have permitted these kind of pencils to accumulate on our shelves, knowing we can sell them at a profit of five cents apiece any time we choose. 13.____

14. Believing that you will want an unexagerated estimate of the amount of business we can expect, I have made every effort to secure accurate figures. 14.____

15. Each and every man, woman and child in that untrameled wilderness carry guns for protection against the wild animals. 15.____

16. Although this process is different than the one to which he is accustomed, a good chemist will have no trouble. 16.____

17. Insensible to the fuming and fretting going on about him, the engineer continued to drive the mammoth dynamo to its utmost capacity. 17.____

18. Everyone had studied his lesson carefully and was consequently well prepared when the instructor began to discuss the fourth dimention. 18.____

19. I learned Johnny six new arithmetic problems this afternoon. 19.____

20. Athletics is urged by our most prominent citizens as the pursuit which will enable the younger generation to achieve that ideal of education, a sound mind in a sound body. 20.____

21. He did not see whoever was at the door very clearly but thinks it was the city tax appraiser. 21.____

22. He could not scarsely believe that his theories had been substantiated in this convincing fashion. 22.____

23. Although you have displayed great ingenuity in carrying out your assignments, the choice for the position still lies among Brown and Smith. 23.____

24. If they had have pleaded at the time that Smith was an accessory to the crime, it would have lessened the punishment. 24.____

25. It has proven indispensible in his compilation of the facts in the matter. 25.____

KEY (CORRECT ANSWERS)

1. A
2. D
3. B
4. D
5. B
6. A
7. D
8. C
9. C
10. A
11. A
12. D
13. C
14. B
15. D
16. C
17. A
18. B
19. C
20. A
21. B
22. D
23. C
24. D
25. B

TEST 3

Questions 1-5.

DIRECTIONS: Questions 1 through 5 consist of sentences which may or may not contain errors in grammar or spelling or both. Sentences which do not contain errors in grammar or spelling or both are to be considered correct, even though there may be other correct ways of expressing the same thought. Examine each sentence carefully. Then, in the space at the right, write the letter of the answer which is the BEST of those suggested below:

A. If the sentence is correct;
B. If the sentence contains an error in spelling;
C. If the sentence contains an error in grammar;
D. If the sentence contains errors in both grammar and spelling.

1. Brown is doing fine although the work is irrevelant to his training. 1.____

2. The conference of sales managers voted to set its adjournment at one o'clock in order to give those present an opportunity to get rid of all merchandise. 2.____

3. He decided that in view of what had taken place at the hotel that he ought to stay and thank the benificent stranger who had rescued him from an embarassing situation. 3.____

4. Since you object to me criticizing your letter, I have no alternative but to consider you a mercenary scoundrel. 4.____

5. I rushed home ahead of schedule so that you will leave me go to the picnic with Mary. 5.____

Questions 6-15.

DIRECTIONS: Some of the following sentences contain an error in spelling, word usage, or sentence structure, or punctuation. Some sentences are correct as they stand although there may be other correct ways of expressing the same thought. All incorrect sentences contain only one error. Mark your answer to each question in the space at the right as follows:

A. If the sentence has an error in spelling;
B. If the sentence has an error in punctuation or capitalization;
C. If the sentence has an error in word usage or sentence structure;
D. If the sentence is correct.

6. Because the chairman failed to keep the participants from wandering off into irrelevant discussions, it was impossible to reach a consensus before the meeting was adjourned. 6.____

7. Certain employers have an unwritten rule that any applicant, who is over 55 years of age, is automatically excluded from consideration for any position whatsoever. 7.____

8. If the proposal to build schools in some new apartment buildings were to be accepted by the builders, one of the advantages that could be expected to result would be better communication between teachers and parents of schoolchildren. 8.____

9. In this instance, the manufacturer's violation of the law against deseptive packaging was discernible only to an experienced inspector. 9.____

10. The tenants' anger stemmed from the president's going to Washington to testify without consulting them first. 10.____

11. Did the president of this eminent banking company say; "We intend to hire and train a number of these disadvan-taged youths?" 11.____

12. In addition, today's confidential secretary must be knowledgable in many different areas: for example, she must know modern techniques for making travel arrangements for the executive. 12.____

13. To avoid further disruption of work in the offices, the protesters were forbidden from entering the building unless they had special passes. 13.____

14. A valuable secondary result of our training conferences is the opportunities afforded for management to observe the reactions of the participants. 14.____

15. Of the two proposals submitted by the committee, the first one is the best. 15.____

Questions 16-25.

DIRECTIONS: Each of the following sentences may be classified MOST appropriately under one of the following three categories:

A. Faulty because of incorrect grammar
B. Faulty because of incorrect punctuation
C. Correct

Examine each sentence. Then, print the capital letter preceding the BEST choice of the three suggested above. All incorrect sentences contain only one type of error. Consider a sentence correct if it contains none of the types of errors mentioned, even though there may be other ways of expressing the same thought.

16. He sent the notice to the clerk who you hired yesterday. 16.____

17. It must be admitted, however that you were not informed of this change. 17.____

18. Only the employees who have served in this grade for at least two years are eligible for promotion. 18.____

19. The work was divided equally between she and Mary. 19.____

20. He thought that you were not available at that time. 20.____

21. When the messenger returns; please give him this package. 21.____

22. The new secretary prepared, typed, addressed, and delivered, the notices. 22.____

23. Walking into the room, his desk can be seen at the rear. 23.____

24. Although John has worked here longer than she, he produces a smaller amount of work. 24.____

25. She said she could of typed this report yesterday. 25.____

KEY (CORRECT ANSWERS)

1. D
2. A
3. D
4. C
5. C
6. A
7. B
8. D
9. A
10. D
11. B
12. A
13. C
14. D
15. C
16. A
17. B
18. C
19. A
20. C
21. B
22. B
23. A
24. C
25. A

TEST 4

Questions 1-5.

DIRECTIONS: Each of the following sentences may be classified MOST appropriately under one of the following three categories:

A. Faulty because of incorrect grammar
B. Faulty because of incorrect punctuation
C. Correct

Examine each sentence. Then, print the capital letter preceding the BEST choice of the three suggested above. All incorrect sentences contain only one type of error. Consider a sentence correct if it contains none of the types of errors mentioned, even though there may be other correct ways of expressing the same thought.

1. Neither one of these procedures are adequate for the efficient performance of this task. 1.____

2. The typewriter is the tool of the typist; the cash register, the tool of the cashier. 2.____

3. "The assignment must be completed as soon as possible" said the supervisor. 3.____

4. As you know, office handbooks are issued to all new employees. 4.____

5. Writing a speech is sometimes easier than to deliver it before an audience. 5.____

Questions 6-15.

DIRECTIONS: Each statement given in Questions 6 through 15 contains one of the faults of English usage listed below. For each, choose from the options listed the MAJOR fault contained.

A. The statement is not a complete sentence.
B. The statement contains a word or phrase that is redundant.
C. The statement contains a long, less commonly used word when a shorter, more direct word would be acceptable.
D. The statement contains a colloquial expression that normally is avoided in business writing.

6. The fact that this activity will afford an opportunity to meet your group. 6.____

7. Do you think that the two groups can join together for next month's meeting? 7.____

8. This is one of the most exciting new innovations to be introduced into our college. 8.____

9. We expect to consummate the agenda before the meeting ends tomorrow at noon. 9.____

10. While this seminar room is small in size, we think we can use it. 10.____

11. Do you think you can make a modification in the date of the Budget Committee meeting? 11.____

12. We are cognizant of the problem but we think we can ameliorate the situation. 12.____

13. Shall I call you around three on the day I arrive in the City? 13.____

14. Until such time that we know precisely that the students will be present. 14.____

15. The consensus of opinion of all the members present is reported in the minutes. 15.____

Questions 16-25.

DIRECTIONS: For each of Questions 16 through 25, select from the options given below the MOST applicable choice.

A. The sentence is correct.
B. The sentence contains a spelling error only.
C. The sentence contains an English grammar error only.
D. The sentence contains both a spelling error and an English grammar error.

16. Every person in the group is going to do his share. 16.____

17. The man who we selected is new to this University. 17.____

18. She is the older of the four secretaries on the two staffs that are to be combined. 18.____

19. The decision has to be made between him and I. 19.____

20. One of the volunteers are too young for this complecated task, don't you think? 20.____

21. I think your idea is splindid and it will improve this report considerably. 21.____

22. Do you think this is an exagerated account of the behavior you and me observed this morning? 22.____

23. Our supervisor has a clear idea of excelence. 23.____

24. How many occurences were verified by the observers? 24.____

25. We must complete the typing of the draft of the questionaire by noon tomorrow. 25.____

KEY (CORRECT ANSWERS)

1. A
2. C
3. B
4. C
5. A

6. A
7. B
8. B
9. C
10. B

11. C
12. C
13. D
14. A
15. B

16. A
17. C
18. C
19. C
20. D

21. B
22. D
23. B
24. B
25. B

PREPARING WRITTEN MATERIALS

EXAMINATION SECTION
TEST 1

DIRECTIONS: Each question contains a sentence. Read each sentence carefully to decide whether it is correct. Then, in the space at the right, mark your answer:

A. If the sentence is incorrect because of bad grammar or sentence structure;
B. If the sentence is incorrect because of bad punctuation;
C. If the sentence is incorrect because of bad capitalization;
D. If the sentence is correct.

Each incorrect sentence has only one type of error. Consider a sentence correct if it has no errors, although there may be other correct ways of saying the same thing.

<u>SAMPLE QUESTION I</u>; One of our clerks were promoted yesterday.

The subject of this sentence is *one,* so the verb should be *was promoted* instead of *were promoted.* Since the sentence is incorrect because of bad grammar, the answer to Sample Question I is A.

<u>SAMPLE QUESTION II</u>: Between you and me, I would prefer not going there.

Since this sentence is correct, the answer to Sample Question II is D.

1. The National alliance of Businessmen is trying to persuade private businesses to hire youth in the summertime. 1._____

2. The supervisor who is on vacation, is in charge of processing vouchers. 2._____

3. The activity of the committee at its conferences is always stimulating. 3._____

4. After checking the addresses again, the letters went to the mailroom. 4._____

5. The director, as well as the employees, are interested in sharing the dividends. 5._____

6. The experiments conducted by professor Alford were described at a recent meeting of our organization. 6._____

7. I shall be glad to discuss these matters with whoever represents the Municipal Credit Union. 7._____

8. In my opinion, neither Mr. Price nor Mr. Roth knows how to operate this office appliance. 8._____

9. The supervisor, as well as the other stenographers, were unable to transcribe Miss Johnson's shorthand notes. 9._____

10. Important functions such as, recruiting and training, are performed by our unit. 10._____

11. Realizing that many students are interested in this position, we sent announcements to all the High Schools. 11.____

12. After pointing out certain incorrect conclusions, the report was revised by Mr. Clark and submitted to Mr. Batson. 12.____

13. The employer contributed two hundred dollars; the employees, one hundred dollars. 13.____

14. He realized that the time, when a supervisor could hire and fire, was over. 14.____

15. The complaints received by Commissioner Regan was the cause of the change in policy. 15.____

16. Any report, that is to be sent to the Federal Security Administration, must be approved and signed by Mr. Yound. 16.____

17. Of the two stenographers, Miss Rand is the more accurate. 17.____

18. Since the golf courses are crowded during the Summer, more men are needed to maintain the courses in good playing condition. 18.____

19. Although he invited Mr. Frankel and I to attend a meeting of the Civil Service Assembly, we were unable to accept his invitation. 19.____

20. Only the employees who worked overtime last week may leave one hour earlier today. 20.____

21. We need someone who can speak french fluently. 21.____

22. A tall, elderly, man entered the office and asked to see Mr. Brown. 22.____

23. The clerk insisted that he had filed the correspondence in the proper cabinet. 23.____

24. "Will you assist us," he asked? 24.____

25. According to the information contained in the report, a large quantity of paper and envelopes were used by this bureau last year. 25.____

KEY (CORRECT ANSWERS)

1. C
2. B
3. D
4. A
5. A
6. C
7. D
8. D
9. A
10. B
11. C
12. A
13. D
14. B
15. A
16. B
17. D
18. C
19. A
20. D
21. C
22. B
23. D
24. B
25. A

TEST 2

DIRECTIONS: Each question consists of a sentence which may be classified appropriately under one of the following four categories:

A. Incorrect because of faulty grammar or sentence structure;
B. Incorrect because of faulty punctuation;
C. Incorrect because of faulty capitalization;
D. Correct

Examine each sentence carefully. Then, in the space at the right, print the capital letter preceding the option which is the BEST of the four suggested above. All incorrect sentences contain only one type of error. Consider a sentence correct if it contains none of the types of errors mentioned, although there may be other correct ways of expressing the same thought.

1. Mrs. Black the supervisor of the unit, has many important duties. 1.____

2. We spoke to the man whom you saw yesterday. 2.____

3. When a holiday falls on Sunday, it is officially celebrated on monday. 3.____

4. Of the two reports submitted, this one is the best. 4.____

5. Each staff member, including the accountants, were invited to the meeting. 5.____

6. Give the package to whomever calls for it. 6.____

7. To plan the work is our responsibility; to carry it out is his. 7.____

8. "May I see the person in charge of this office," asked the visitor? 8.____

9. He knows that it was not us who prepared the report. 9.____

10. These problems were brought to the attention of senator Johnson. 10.____

11. The librarian classifies all books periodicals and documents. 11.____

12. Any employee who uses an adding machine realizes its importance. 12.____

13. Instead of coming to the office, the clerk should of come to the supply room. 13.____

14. He asked, "will your staff assist us?" 14.____

15. Having been posted on the bulletin board, we were certain that the announcements would be read. 15.____

16. He was not informed, that he would have to work overtime. 16.____

17. The wind blew several papers off of his desk. 17.____

18. Charles Dole, who is a member of the committee, was asked to confer with commissioner Wilson. 18.____

19. Miss Bell will issue a copy to whomever asks for one. 19.____

20. Most employees, and he is no exception do not like to work overtime. 20.____

21. This is the man whom you interviewed last week. 21.____

22. Of the two cities visited, White Plains is the cleanest. 22.____

23. Although he was willing to work on other holidays, he refused to work on Labor day. 23.____

24. If an employee wishes to attend the conference, he should fill out the necessary forms. 24.____

25. The division chief reports that an engineer and an inspector is needed for this special survey. 25.____

KEY (CORRECT ANSWERS)

1. B
2. D
3. C
4. A
5. A

6. A
7. D
8. B
9. A
10. C

11. B
12. D
13. A
14. C
15. A

16. B
17. A
18. C
19. A
20. B

21. D
22. A
23. C
24. D
25. A

TEST 3

DIRECTIONS: Each question consists of a sentence which may be classified appropriately under one of the following four categories:

A. Incorrect because of faulty grammar or sentence structure;
B. Incorrect because of faulty punctuation;
C. Incorrect because of faulty capitalization;
D. Correct

Examine each sentence carefully. Then, in the space at the right, indicate the letter preceding the category which is the BEST of the four suggested above. Each incorrect sentence contains only one type of error. Consider a sentence correct if it contains none of the types of errors mentioned, although there may be other correct ways of expressing the same thought.

1. We have learned that there was more than twelve people present at the meeting. 1._____

2. Every one of the employees is able to do this kind of work. 2._____

3. Neither the supervisor nor his assistant are in the office today. 3._____

4. The office manager announced that any clerk, who volunteered for the assignment, would be rewarded. 4._____

5. After looking carefully in all the files, the letter was finally found on a desk. 5._____

6. In answer to the clerk's question, the supervisor said, "this assignment must be completed today." 6._____

7. The office manager says that he can permit only you and me to go to the meeting. 7._____

8. The supervisor refused to state who he would assign to the reception unit. 8._____

9. At the last meeting, he said that he would interview us in September. 9._____

10. Mr. Jones, who is one of our most experienced employees has been placed in charge of the main office. 10._____

11. I think that this adding machine is the most useful of the two we have in our office. 11._____

12. Between you and I, our new stenographer is not as competent as our former stenographer. 12._____

13. The new assignment should be given to whoever can do the work rapidly. 13._____

14. Mrs. Smith, as well as three other typists, was assigned to the new office. 14._____

15. The staff assembled for the conference on time but, the main speaker arrived late. 15._____

16. The work was assigned to Miss Green and me. 16._____

17. The staff regulations state that an employee, who is frequently tardy, may receive a negative evaluation. 17._____

18. He is the kind of person who is always willing to undertake difficult assignments. 18._____

19. Mr. Wright's request cannot be granted under no conditions. 19.____

20. George Colt a new employee, was asked to deliver the report to the Domestic Relations Court. 20.____

21. The supervisor entered the room and said, "The work must be completed today." 21.____

22. The employees were given their assignments and, they were asked to begin work immediately. 22.____

23. The letter will be sent to the United States senate this week. 23.____

24. When the supervisor entered the room, he noticed that the book was laying on the desk. 24.____

25. The price of the pens were higher than the price of the pencils. 25.____

KEY (CORRECT ANSWERS)

1.	A	11.	A
2.	D	12.	A
3.	A	13.	D
4.	B	14.	D
5.	A	15.	B
6.	C	16.	D
7.	D	17.	B
8.	A	18.	D
9.	C	19.	A
10.	B	20.	B

21. D
22. B
23. C
24. A
25. A

CPSIA information can be obtained
at www.ICGtesting.com
Printed in the USA
BVHW060007250522
637944BV00006B/249

9 781731 849953